Encounters *avec l'Autre* in Contemporary Montreal Literature

Aspects of Francophone-Anglophone Interactions
at the Turn of the New Millennium

Stefanie Rudig

Stefanie Rudig

Encounters *avec l'Autre* in Contemporary Montreal Literature

Aspects of Francophone-Anglophone Interactions
at the Turn of the New Millennium

ibidem-Verlag
Stuttgart

Bibliografische Information der Deutschen Nationalbibliothek
Die Deutsche Nationalbibliothek verzeichnet diese Publikation in der Deutschen Nationalbibliografie; detaillierte bibliografische Daten sind im Internet über http://dnb.d-nb.de abrufbar.

Bibliographic information published by the Deutsche Nationalbibliothek
Die Deutsche Nationalbibliothek lists this publication in the Deutsche Nationalbibliografie; detailed bibliographic data are available in the Internet at http://dnb.d-nb.de.

Coverabbildung: "Les trois drapeaux". Fotografie Peter Mertz, Innsbruck. Abdruck mit freundlicher Genehmigung.

∞

Gedruckt auf alterungsbeständigem, säurefreien Papier
Printed on acid-free paper

ISBN-13: 978-3-8382-0243-3

© *ibidem*-Verlag
Stuttgart 2011

Alle Rechte vorbehalten

Das Werk einschließlich aller seiner Teile ist urheberrechtlich geschützt. Jede Verwertung außerhalb der engen Grenzen des Urheberrechtsgesetzes ist ohne Zustimmung des Verlages unzulässig und strafbar. Dies gilt insbesondere für Vervielfältigungen, Übersetzungen, Mikroverfilmungen und elektronische Speicherformen sowie die Einspeicherung und Verarbeitung in elektronischen Systemen.

All rights reserved. No part of this publication may be reproduced, stored in or introduced into a retrieval system, or transmitted, in any form, or by any means (electronic, mechanical, photocopying, recording or otherwise) without the prior written permission of the publisher. Any person who does any unauthorized act in relation to this publication may be liable to criminal prosecution and civil claims for damages.

Printed in Germany

Table of Contents

Acknowledgments 6
List of Illustrations 7
Preface 8
1. Introduction 11
2. Historical and Socio-Cultural Framework 15
    2.1. A Short Eclectic History of English-French Relations in Canada 16
        2.1.1. The French Regime 17
        2.1.2. The British Regime 18
        2.1.3. Quebec – *Une société distincte* 21
    2.2. Language and Identity 101 24
        2.2.1. *Parlo Ergo Sum* 24
        2.2.2. "*Un chiffre que les Montréalais aiment beaucoup*" 26
    2.3. Literary Voices 29
3. Methodological Considerations and Contextualisation 33
    3.1. Montreal – A Doubly Postcolonial City 34
    3.2. Two Contemporary Spokespersons and Their Oeuvre 37
    3.3. Some Reflections on Genre 41
    3.4. Circumstantial History of the Works Discussed 44
4. Contact Zones / *Zones de contact* 49
    4.1. Multiculturalism, Interculturalism and Transculturalism 57
    4.2. Self and Other – Initiation to the Kingdom of Babel 60
    4.3. Montreal's Significant Other(s) 67
    4.4. "*Je me souviens*" – Writing Memory 75
    4.5. A Tale of Two Cities 82
    4.6. Strangers in the Same House 92
    4.7. Between Humility and Epiphany 100
5. Outlook and Conclusion 111
Bibliography 119
Résumé 131

Acknowledgments

I am indebted to Professor Helga Ramsey-Kurz and Professor Ursula Moser for the critical reading of the manuscript. Thanks are also due to Marie Carrière, Robert Dion, Justin Edwards, Louise Ladouceur, Martine-Emmanuelle Lapointe, Pamela Sing and Peter Webb for their help and book recommendations in the initial phase of my research. Furthermore, I need to thank my Canadian friend Olukunle Owolabi for never tiring to discuss his country with me.

List of Illustrations

Fig. 1: Photo of a chair with a quotation from Dany Laferrière
(Stefanie RUDIG. Quebec City, May 2009)

Fig. 2: Cartoon (Quebec History)
(John SAYWELL. *Le Canada hier et aujourd'hui*. Toronto: Irwin, 1985. 64)

Fig. 3: Symbolic value of the number "101" for francophone Quebecers
(André BERNARD. "Les répercussions sociales et politiques de la Loi 101." In *Le Français au Québec: 400 ans d'histoire et de vie*. Ed. Michel Plourde. Québec: Fides, 2003. 294)[*]

Fig. 4: "*Arrêt*/Stop" sign in Quebec, on which the English word "Stop" has been partially effaced and transformed into "101"
(Guy ROCHER. "La politique et la loi linguistiques du Québec en 1977." In *Le Français au Québec: 400 ans d'histoire et de vie*. Ed. Michel Plourde. Québec: Fides, 2003. 277)[*]

Fig. 5: Quebec Coat of Arms
(Jérôme BLUM. "Coat of arms of the province of Quebec." 29 July 2006. *Wikimedia Commons*. 4 Feb. 2011 <http://en.wikipedia.org/wiki/File:Coat_of_arms_of_Qu%C3%A9bec.svg>)

---

[*] Reproduction rights are kindly granted by Éditions Fides.

Preface

Gare centrale - Montréal. "What's 'luggage storage' in French?" I wonder. After having spent a considerable time in the US, English comes to mind more readily. Knowing that Quebec is a French-speaking province and vaguely aware of the English-French dichotomy in Montreal, I hesitantly approach a railway employee. *"Pardon, Monsieur. Parlez-vous anglais?"* "Sometimes, *oui*," he replies with a broad, meaningful grin.

I have always been fascinated by Quebec and by the mere fact that the two languages which I am so passionate about are spoken in this Canadian province. But after this simple, bilingual answer, I instinctively knew that I had to probe deeper into the matter; I had to find out the reasons behind this man's enigmatic smile. My 'journey' led me to write the present study. You are welcome to take a seat and read my results.

Fig. 1
Quebec City, May 2009
© Stefanie Rudig

are we agreed on this my friend
the moon's a word I give to you
and unaccompanied by stars

sommes-nous mon ami d'accord sur ceci
la lune est un mot que je te donne
et sans accompagnement d'étoiles

faisant amitié avec des mots
où le son est le sens
la mésange à capuchon noire
pousse du bec à son bref fi-bi
    deux gouttes de gaieté
    au front de l'hiver

sealing friendship with words
that mean what you hear
the chickadee with its black cap
eases from its beak its soft phee-bee
    two drops of gaiety
    on winter's temples[1]

---

[1] E.D. Blodgett and Jacques Brault. *Transfiguration*. Saint-Lambert, Toronto: Editions du Noroît, Buschek Books, 1999. 40-1 qtd. in Sherry SIMON. *Translating Montreal: Episodes in the Life of a Divided City*. Montreal: McGill-Queen's UP, 2006. 139.

1. Introduction

In a country spared from wars in its recent history, one speaks about 'language wars' and the 'threat' of bilingualism. Quebec – Canada's only province that is officially monolingual francophone – evinces a long obsession with language and language-related anxiety, in particular concerning the survival of the French fact in the hostile context of an overwhelmingly English North America. Quebec's largest and most ethnically and linguistically diverse metropolis, Montreal, is the primary locale for linguistic battles. The city's population is commonly referred to in terms of Francophones,[2] Anglophones and Allophones. To these one has to add the small but persistent 'angryphone' faction, frequently victims of anglophobia who are adverse to linguistic diversity and anything but conducive to language peace in Montreal.

Given the country's political history, the English-French dichotomy is firmly rooted in Quebec's culture. The interaction between Francophones and Anglophones since 1763 has been described as "a relationship of co-operation and confrontation."[3] Chapter two provides a framework to situate this relationship historically and in its socio-cultural context. Special emphasis is put on the connection between language and identity, and its particular importance to Quebecers.

There has been lot to commemorate in Quebec in recent years. In 2008 the province celebrated the 400th anniversary of the founding of Quebec City, while 2009 marked the 475th anniversary of Jacques Cartier's arrival on the Gaspé peninsula and thus the very beginning of French colonisation in North America. Moreover, it is about 250 years ago that French Canadians were defeated by the British in a decisive battle and were subsequently transformed into a *peuple vaincu*, the consciousness of which Quebec's Francophones could not easily shake off for centuries. Much attention – academic and non-academic alike – has been paid to the evolution of French-English relations in Quebec. But what does the situation look like today, more than half a century after the publication of Hugh MacLennan's *Two Solitudes*, Canada's paradigmatic novel about the country's two major language communities? Literary studies that are devoted to this subject and that examine books published within the

---

[2] In this study the term 'Francophone' is used to denote a person whose first language is French; it does not include an ethnic dimension, that is, 'Francophone' does not necessarily refer to a Quebecer of French (Canadian) ancestry. The same holds true for the 'Anglophone' equivalent.

[3] Jocelyn LÉTOURNEAU. *A History for the Future: Rewriting Memory and Identity in Quebec*. Montreal: McGill-Queen's UP, 2004. 134.

last ten to fifteen years are rare. Yet, decades after such pivotal events in Québécois history as the Quiet Revolution, the October crisis, the passing of Bill 101 – the province's most important piece of language legislation to date – and the two referenda on independence, the state of French-English relations seems to call for a re-evaluation. This study seeks to investigate the status-quo of the anglophone-francophone dynamic in Quebec's social laboratory, that is Montreal, on the basis of selected works by Monique Proulx and Neil Bissoondath, two authors who presently live and write in Quebec. Since the subject of the 'two solitudes' is extremely vast, the reasons why the present study has been narrowed down to its specific selection of authors and texts are explained in chapter three.

Montreal is in a process of transformation. In his history of the city since Confederation, Paul-André Linteau declares in 2000, "*La métropole affiche un dynamisme nouveau et un air de prospérité qui tranchent avec la morosité du début de la décennie. Elle entre avec optimisme dans le 21e siècle.*"[4] This optimism can well be extended with regard to the city's language duality. Several signs indicate a growing rapprochement between the two language groups and former historical rivals. By drawing on literary voices from both sides of the linguistic divide, chapter four analyses how Francophones and Anglophones encounter and interact with the Other in fiction published shortly before and after the turn of the twenty-first century. Montreal scholar Sherry Simon argues that it is "in the city's contact zones […] that the reality of contemporary Montreal is most strikingly expressed."[5] Chapter four, the main part of the analysis, reads contemporary Montreal literature as a contact zone and traces the characters' experiences there. Furthermore, it highlights that, while the English-French binarism was for a long time the "main event in the embattled city,"[6] the situation today is more complex, as immigrants have become a third partner in the relationship of Montreal's legendary 'two solitudes.'

The last part of this study comes to a conclusion by also taking a brief look at the situation between the two major linguistic communities in Montreal beyond the realm of literature. Chapter five thus discusses in how far the literary representations reflect the present-day reality and whether there really is increasing contact and dia-

---

[4] Paul-André LINTEAU. *Histoire de Montréal depuis la Confédération.* 2e éd. Montréal: Boréal, 2000. 568.
[5] Moreover, Simon continues by writing that "the city has turned certain historically charged frontiers of distrust into zones of creativity" (SIMON (2006), 212).
[6] SIMON (2006), 56.

logue between Francophones and Anglophones about fifteen years after Quebec almost seceded from Canada.

2. Historical and Socio-Cultural Framework

It is essential to place the present discussion in its historical context in order to grasp the intricacies of English-French relations in Canada, in particular with regard to Quebec, where present-day animosities are to a great extent due to past hostilities. History continues to haunt French and English Canadians; a comparative study of Canadian history textbooks published between 1954 and 1964 for use in francophone and anglophone schools, for instance, concludes that "the two sets of authors are not even writing the history of the same country."[7] While it is important not to downplay the tensions between Anglophones and Francophones, Jocelyn Létourneau argues against transmitting a "heritage of resentment," because "it would wreck the future rather than build it."[8] Yet a sense of the past is indispensable for a nation's collective memory as much as for a personal one, or as the narrator of Neil Bissoondath's novel *Doing the Heart Good* puts it, "We do owe [our children] a sense of our and their yesterdays."[9]

Fig. 2

---

[7] Qtd. in Eva-Marie KRÖLLER. "Introduction." In *The Cambridge Companion to Canadian Literature*. Ed. Eva-Marie Kröller. Cambridge: Cambridge UP, 2004. 12.

[8] LÉTOURNEAU, 127.

[9] Neil BISSOONDATH. *Doing the Heart Good*. London: Scribner, 2002. 268 (forthwith abbreviated as *DHG*).

Conflicts between the country's two white settler colonies were not only about territory but also about language. Quebec has consequently been a society transformed[10] from one speaking French to one using English, before becoming predominantly francophone and multilingual. Language being so intimately tied up with identity, necessitated for Franco-Quebecers that French should be protected and promoted by law in order to regain its vitality. As a result of the tenacious struggle of French Canadians, Francophones are now again a confident majority in Quebec and thus have maintained their visibility (and audibility) in North America. All the while writers have been contributing creatively to the debate and shaping it to an extent anything but insignificant.

2.1. A Short Eclectic History of English-French Relations in Canada

> The history of Canada can be told in many ways: [...] For the British the history of Canada must be seen as largely a success story [...]. For the French it is quite different. For them it is a story of colonial adventure followed by defeat in 1758, and then years of passive and not so passive resistance to the victorious power during which they preserved their church, their language and their culture until they were able to assert themselves both politically and culturally as equal partners in a country which many of them now wish to leave.[11]

The statement quoted above draws attention to the ambivalence inherent in any history of Canada, for indeed there is no such thing as *a* Canadian history; only through a pluralistic approach can one truly fathom the complex and often contradictory histories of Canada. While the present study focuses exclusively on the respective and overlapping histories of the so-called Founding Nations, it does in no way want to disclaim the rich legacy of the First Nations people.

---

[10] The province experienced enormous transformations in other respects within the last century. Jacques Dufresne writes in 1995: "On y parle les deux langues qui ont le plus contribué à faire le monde tel qu'il est aujourd'hui. La société de ce Québec était traditionnelle, médiévale même, il y a à peine cinquante ans ; elle devance aujourd'hui la Californie dans certaines expérimentations, ou en tout cas elle la suit toujours de très prés. " (Jacques DUFRESNE. "Le Québec, cobaye et définisseur de la mondialisation." *Grenzgänge* 3 (1995): 11).

[11] Coral Ann HOWELLS. Ed. *Where are the Voices Coming From? Canadian Culture and the Legacies of History*. Amsterdam, NY: Rodopi, 2004. xi.

2.1.1. The French Regime

Jacques Cartier's arrival in Gaspé in 1534 marked the beginning of the French colonial adventure in the New World. Treating the land like a *terra nullius* and ignoring that the Amerindians had inhabited the territory of Quebec for some 10,000 to 40,000 years,[12] he claimed possession of what he called *la Nouvelle France* in the name of the King of France, François I. The latter, however, initially showed little interest in his new colony, because he was disappointed in Cartier, whom he had commissioned to find a new passage to Asia and its riches such as gold and spices. It was not until the beginning of the seventeenth century that Quebec attracted the attention of the French crown and that a true and sustained colonisation of the territory began. This development coincided with the founding of Quebec City, the first French settlement in North America and first permanent settlement in Canada,[13] by Samuel de Champlain[14] in 1608, and the increasing importance of the fur and fishing trade.[15]

Almost since its very foundation, Quebec, generally labelled the cradle of French civilisation on the North American continent, was subject to military attacks from the English. Even years before the North American colonial wars between Great Britain and France (1689-1763) began, the territory of Quebec fell into British possession, as it was seized by English privateers led by Sir David Kirke in 1629, only to be returned to France three years later.[16] Moreover, the British allied themselves with the Iroquois and continued to attack French establishments throughout the century. In 1701, the Great Peace of Montreal put an end to nearly a hundred years of war be-

---

[12] Cf. Jean PROVENCHER. *Chronologie du Québec 1534-2000*. Montréal: Boréal, 2000. 15.

[13] On the occasion of the 400th anniversary of Quebec City in 2008 Prime Minister Stephen Harper affirmed, "It is an [*sic*] historic date for all of Canada and for North America. On that date, we truly began to become what we are today. For the founding of Quebec also marks the founding of the Canadian state." (OFFICE OF THE PRIME MINISTER. "Prime Minister Addresses Francophonie Summit." 2006. 17 Aug. 2009 <http://pm.gc.ca/eng/ media.asp?category=2&id=1338>.)

[14] Champlain entered history as the Father of New France, "*le père de la Nouvelle-France*" (Nicole MAURY and Jules TESSIER. *A l'écoute des francophones d'Amérique*. Montréal: Centre éducatif et culturel, 1991. 35).

[15] Cf. Bernhard PÖLL. *Francophonies périphériques: Histoire, statut et profil des principales variétés du français hors de France*. Paris: L'Harmattan, 2001. 101, 103. See also: Jacques MATHIEU. "La naissance d'un nouveau monde." In *Le Français au Québec: 400 ans d'histoire et de vie*. Ed. Michel Plourde. Québec: Fides, 2003. 5-6.

[16] Cf. PÖLL, 104. See also: Jacques MATHIEU. "New France." *The Canadian Encyclopedia*. 2009. Historica Foundation of Canada. 17 Aug. 2009 <http://www.thecanadianencyclopedia.com/ index.cfm?PgNm=TCE&Params=A1ARTA0005701>.

tween New France and the Five Nations Iroquois, who agreed to remain neutral in any subsequent conflicts between the French and British colonies.[17]

The eighteenth century witnessed pivotal transformations in the power struggle between the two colonial forces in Canada. Under the terms of the Treaty of Utrecht, France was first forced to cede Acadia, Newfoundland and the Hudson Bay to Britain in 1713. Yet, the greatest blow to French Canadians happened in 1759, when the troops of the Marquis de Montcalm were defeated by those of General Wolfe in the Battle of the Plains of Abraham. Through the signing of the Treaty of Paris, which officially ended the Seven Years' War (1756-1763), France lost almost all of its North American possessions to Britain and King George III renamed his new Canadian colony the "Province of Quebec" by Royal Proclamation issued on October 7, 1763.[18] This marked the end of the period of *La Nouvelle France* and while French political power in America was virtually non-existent afterwards, the French legacy and presence on the continent has continued to this day.

2.1.2. The British Regime

As a result of the Treaty of Paris the structure of Canada's society underwent profound changes. During the years following the British Conquest a considerable number of French Canadians, including the military personnel, administrators and merchants, returned to France; those who chose to stay were for the most part economically marginalised and ruined,[19] and it was not until the nineteenth century that a new francophone professional middle class emerged. The sudden political and economic void was immediately filled by the British (colonial) rulers[20] and English became the dominant language (in the public domain) in a country where Francophones constituted the significant majority of the population. In his travel diary *Voyage en Amérique* (engl.: *Journey to America*) the French intellectual Alexis de Tocqueville observes the following in 1831:

> Le fond de la population et l'immense majorité sont partout français. Mais il est facile de voir que les Français sont le peuple vaincu. Les classes riches appartiennent pour la plupart à la race anglaise. Bien que le français soit la langue presque universellement parlée, la plu-

---

[17] Cf. PROVENCHER, 80.
[18] Cf. MATHIEU (2009); PROVENCHER, 114-15.
[19] This point does not apply to the peasantry, because for them there was probably not much difference in their economic well-being under French or British rule.
[20] Those were later joined by the tens of thousands of American loyalists who settled in Canada after the American War of Independence.

part des journaux, les affiches, et jusqu'aux enseignes des marchands français sont en anglais ! Les entreprises commerciales sont presque toutes en leurs mains. C'est véritablement la classe dirigeante du Canada.[21]

The new Province of Quebec was thus faced with the task of finding an acceptable mode of co-existence between its two major linguistic groups and historical rivals, whose relationship in the beginning could be said to have been "tense yet cordial."[22]

In 1774, the Quebec Act was passed, which officially recognised the French language, re-established French civil law at the same time as British common law, granted Catholics the right to practise their religion and allowed Canadians of French origin to hold office in the government.[23] These measures were on the one hand intended to rectify some of the problems simmering since the Royal Proclamation of 1763, and on the other to ensure the loyalty of the colony's French Catholics at a time not long before France would announce its support to the American colonies in their War of Independence.

The British Parliament adopted another Act in 1791, the Constitutional Act, which divided the country into two colonies: Upper Canada, which was predominantly English-speaking and which corresponded approximately to present-day Ontario, and the largely francophone Lower Canada that would eventually become today's Quebec.[24] For some scholars the Constitutional Act presented the first step on the path that would lead towards the Confederation debates of the 1860s, while others see its failure to establish a responsible government as another factor exacerbating the political conflicts of the early nineteenth century.[25]

In 1837/38, the French Canadians of Lower Canada attempted an insurrection (also known as the Patriots' Rebellion) against British Crown rule but failed. In its aftermath Lord Durham was sent for to analyse the situation in Canada. He does so remarking in his *Report on the Affairs of British North America* (1839):

> I expected to find a contest between a government and a people: I found two nations warring in the bosom of a single state: I found a struggle, not of principles, but of races; and I

---

[21] Qtd. in PÖLL, 104.
[22] M.D. BEHIELS. "Francophone-Anglophone Relations." *The Canadian Encyclopedia*. 2009. Historica Foundation of Canada. 17 Aug. 2009 <http://www.thecanadianencyclopedia.com/ index.cfm?PgNm= TCE&Params=A1SEC820892>.
[23] Cf. PROVENCHER, 121.
[24] However, the constitutional text remains silent on matters regarding language and religion (cf. Denis VAUGEOIS. "Une langue sans statut." In *Le Français au Québec: 400 ans d'histoire et de vie*. Ed. Michel Plourde. Québec: Fides, 2003. 65-66).
[25] Cf. PROVENCHER, 129. See also: Pierre TOUSIGNANT. "Constitutional Act, 1791." *The Canadian Encyclopedia*. 2009. Historica Foundation of Canada. 17 Aug. 2009 <http://www.thecanadianencyclopedia.com/index.cfm?PgNm=TCE&Params=A1ARTA0001872>.

perceived that it would be idle to attempt any amelioration of laws or institutions until we could first succeed in terminating the deadly animosity that now separates the inhabitants of Lower Canada into the hostile divisions of French and English.[26]

His two main recommendations – responsible government and the union of Upper and Lower Canada – were followed and the two provinces were merged into the Province of (United) Canada through the Act of Union in 1840. The francophone population was thus put into a minority position and English was declared the only official language of United Canada, which was, however, revised eight years later in favour of bilingualism.[27] The aim underlying these developments, together with widespread immigration from Britain, was a gradual assimilation of French Canadians into British culture. Yet, Francophones were not to be supplanted by Anglophones, at least not in number. Their birth rates, which, well into the twentieth century, were extraordinarily high, allowed them to provide the necessary demographic counterbalance, nowadays commonly referred to as *la revanche des berceaux* ("the revenge of the cradle").[28]

The Canadian state in its modern federal structure was born in 1867, as the Constitution Act (also called British North America Act) united the four provinces Ontario, Quebec, New Brunswick and Nova Scotia to form the Dominion of Canada. Section 133 of the Act guaranteed bilingualism in federal and Quebec parliaments, courts and tribunals.[29] At that time it was clear that 'federation' meant a union of Canada's two founding nations, but this, among other things, would be heatedly discussed in the following century. Especially in the late 1980s/early 1990s the constitutional debates seemed to reach a climax, when Quebec called for a reform of the constitution and the acknowledgment of its special status as a *société distincte* ("distinct society") and as one of Canada's two founding peoples (not just one of the country's ten equal provinces). The province's attempts failed, however, as neither

---

[26] Lord Durham qtd. in J.M. BLISS. Ed. *Canadian History in Documents: 1763-1966*. Toronto: Ryerson Press, 1966. 50.

[27] Cf. Ingo KOLBOOM and Paul LÉTOURNEAU. "Québec zwischen Integration und Souveränität: Ein kanadisches Dilemma." *Grenzgänge* 3 (1995): 29. See also: PÖLL, 105.

[28] The population of French origin in Lower Canada multiplied by ten between 1763 and 1851, counting 696 000 inhabitants. Due to immigration the number of inhabitants of British origin in Lower Canada increased rapidly at the beginning of the nineteenth century, constituting a quarter of the total population of Lower Canada in 1851. In Upper Canada the population counted hardly 10 000 inhabitants in 1791, but exceeded that of Lower Canada by the middle of the nineteenth century because of an important wave of immigration, notably in the 1840s (cf. John A. DICKINSON. "L'anglicisation." In *Le Français au Québec: 400 ans d'histoire et de vie*. Ed. Michel Plourde. Québec: Fides, 2003. 85).

[29] Cf. PROVENCHER, 173.

the Meech Lake (1987/90) nor the Charlottetown Accord (1992) – two amendments to the Canadian Constitution meant to make it acceptable to Quebec – were ratified.[30]

2.1.3. Quebec – *Une société distincte*

The previous sections summarise the main developments in the history of anglophone-francophone relations up to Confederation. In general, conflicts in the nineteenth century evolved around religion, which appeared to have been even more of a divide than language, education (e.g. the Manitoba Schools Question in the late 1890s) and language; and quite interestingly, though also quite obviously, even the question of actual territorial sovereignty seems to have been subordinated to the question of language. The co-existence of four big ethnic groups (French, English, Scottish and Irish) and two different linguistic blocks on the same territory did not go without creating multiple tensions that erupted from time to time, but somehow the groups managed to elaborate, as the historian Paul-André Linteau puts it, a sort of "*pacte tacite de non-agression.*"[31] Without wanting to oversimplify the course of events as it evolved in the twentieth century, this section concentrates on those developments and turning points in the English-French dichotomy since the *Révolution tranquille* ("Quiet Revolution") that are most pertinent to the purpose of this study and which have shaped contemporary Quebec's society.

Numerous factors[32] contributed to the rise of a new Quebec nationalism that reached its first culmination point in the 1960s. Yet, what it primarily stemmed from was the fact that Quebec's Francophones felt like second-class citizens in their own country. Since English was the language of the public domain, including the work place, the French-speaking population had difficulties climbing the social ladder and were effectively discriminated against, so they revolted.

What is known as *la Révolution tranquille* is a period of radical but peaceful upheavals (hence *Quiet* Revolution) in Quebec. The victory of the Liberal Party under Jean Lesage in 1960 precipitated roughly a decade of profound restructuring and

---

[30] Cf. KOLBOOM and LETOURNEAU, 31-32.
[31] LINTEAU, 48.
[32] Worth noting are the particularly acrimonious dispute over the issue of conscription during WWI, the independence of Canada from Britain with the passage of the *Statute of Westminster* (1931), and the post-WWII period of *la grande noirceur* during the Duplessis era (1945-59), which was a time of extremely conservative government as the Union Nationale Party dominated Quebec's political scene, but also of economic growth that brought about the rise of a new (francophone) middle class, urbanisation and rural exodus.

modernisation of Quebec's society. In accordance with Lesage's slogan – "*C'est le temps que ça change!*" – the Party undertook a number of reforms: the secularisation of the education system (and ultimately of society), the partial redistribution of economic power to Francophones by the nationalisation of the province's hydroelectric companies and an expansion of the service sector, and developments in social welfare and health services.[33]

Not only did the Revolution involve struggles over politics and economy, it was above all about language and identity, laying the foundations for an essentially French-speaking Quebec. Embracing the new philosophy "*Maîtres chez nous!*" ("Masters in our own house!"),[34] the nation's francophone majority sought to re-evaluate its role within both the province and Canada, and to define a specific *Québécois* identity. Hand in hand with a revalorisation of the Quebec state and the French language, the francophone population ceased to perceive themselves as French Canadians and developed a Québécois consciousness. However, the term 'Québécois' or 'Quebecer' does no longer solely denote a French-speaking inhabitant of Quebec; instead today's definition of a Quebec identity is now inclusive and based on citizenship ("A Quebecer is someone who lives in Quebec").[35]

At the same time the province saw the emergence of early sovereignty aspirations, but also of nationalist violence, as the first bombs planted by the *Front de libération du Québec* (FLQ)[36] went off in 1963. In 1967, French President Charles de Gaulle's notorious "*Vive le Québec libre!*" speech from the balcony of Montreal's City Hall further fuelled Quebec's independentist movement. In the following year René Lévesque founded the *Parti Québécois*, an advocator of Quebec sovereigntism, while the Montreal-born and pro-federal Pierre Elliott Trudeau became Prime Minis-

---

[33] Cf. LINTEAU, 474-75 and PÖLL, 107.
[34] Qtd. in Peter KLAUS. "Frankophone und Allophone in Québec: *même combat*? Sprache und Literatur als komplementäre Identitätsparadigmata." *Grenzgänge* 3 (1995): 126. For a discussion of language and identity see chapter 2.2.
[35] In contrast to the still "too widely held view according to which being a Quebecer means: 'old-stock French-speaking Quebecer' or Quebecer of French Canadian origin." (Bloc Québécois qtd. in Leigh OAKES and Jane WARREN. *Language, Citizenship and Identity in Quebec*. Basingstoke: Palgrave Macmillan, 2007. 15). Denominations referring to a Quebecer of French Canadian descent include *Québécois pure laine* or *francophone de souche*; another (neutral) way to speak of a francophone Quebecer is also *Franco-Québécois* (cf. OAKES and WARREN, 27, 31, 99).
[36] Provencher speaks of "*le terrorisme québécois*", which probably reached its climax in 1970 with the October Crisis that Trudeau ended by invoking the War Measures Act; it was the first and only peacetime usage of the Act and remains somewhat controversial (cf. PROVENCHER, 279, 293).

ter of Canada.[37] After the events surrounding the October Crisis in 1970, the relationship between Canada and Quebec was put to a further test in 1980, when the Parti Québécois government organised a referendum on Quebec independence with the result that about 60% opposed secession from Canada. Lévesque's "*A la prochaine fois!*" proved to be prophetic as the same scenario more or less repeated itself in 1995; again the sovereigntist cause was defeated, though by a much narrower majority of 50.56% with a participation rate of nearly 94%.[38]

Now nearly fifteen years after the second referendum, things have gone back to a state of normalcy, or say tranquillity, although, as Oakes and Warren noted in 2007, "the question of separation from Canada comes up periodically in the province [...] and it forms part of the backdrop to living in Quebec."[39] In any case, there are several signs for a continuing rapprochement between Anglo- and Franco-Quebecers, so the twenty-first century seems to augur well for overcoming centuries-old animosities between the nation's two founding peoples. In 2005, Canada's newly-appointed Governor General, Haitian-born Montrealer Michaelle Jean, declared,

> Today's world ... demands that we learn to see beyond our wounds, beyond our differences for the good of all [...]. We must eliminate the spectre of all the solitudes and promote solidarity among all the citizens who make up the Canada of today.[40]

To achieve the goal as defined by Governor General Michaelle Jean, it is important not to forget the past but to appropriate it, since "[s]hared understanding of and respect for divergent perceptions of history will be the only way for Canada – or indeed for any country – to survive, let alone evolve, in the twenty-first century."[41]

---

[37] The battle fought on the linguistic front at that time was particularly turbulent and led to a series of crucial language laws in the late 1960s and 1970s (see chapter 2.2.2).
[38] Cf. OAKES and WARREN, 30; PÖLL, 107; PROVENCHER, 286, 313.
[39] OAKES and WARREN, 140.
[40] Qtd. in "The Time of 'Two Solitudes' has passed: Jean." *CTV.ca* 27 Sept. 2005. CTV globe media. 19 Aug. 2009 <http://www.ctv.ca/servlet/ArticleNews/story/CTVNews/20050927/ governor_general_jean_050927/ 20050927?hub=TopStories>.
[41] HOWELLS, 262.

2.2. Language and Identity 101

> To speak a language is to take on a world, a culture.
> - Frantz Fanon[42] -

This section attempts to give a basic introduction to the complex relationship between language and identity, but the number 101 also refers to the most prominent piece of language legislation in Quebec, Bill 101 (1977). Canada, and more specifically Quebec, has proved to be a breeding ground for innovative reflections about language and identity, principally due to its significant francophone and anglophone legacies as outlined in the previous chapters. In fact, the historically enshrined English-French duality in the now officially bilingual country can be said to be as Canadian as the maple leaf. With regard to Quebec, Jean-Ethier Blais further states that *"[p]lus peut-être que partout ailleurs dans le monde, la langue est au Québec un phénomène politique. Elle constitue le baromètre de notre équilibre national."*[43]

2.2.1. Parlo Ergo Sum

The dictum could also be, "I speak French, therefore I am a Quebecer."[44] This was certainly the case at the time of the Quiet Revolution, when the emancipation of Quebec largely happened via language. Today, however, while the French language is still the primary characteristic of Quebec culture, the province's citizens are neither defined ethnically nor linguistically and any discrimination on these grounds has officially been outlawed with the adoption of the Quebec Charter of Human Rights and Freedoms in 1975.[45] In 2001, the Government of Quebec confirmed that "Quebec is a plural society, and French, the official, common language, is a key factor in its social cohesiveness;" this means that everybody is free to choose what language to speak and maintain, but that knowledge of and competence in the French language is vital, especially for immigrants, because in order "to feel at home in Quebec, they will

---

[42] Frantz FANON. *Black Skin, White Masks*. 1952. NY: Grove Press, 1967. 38.
[43] Qtd. in KLAUS, 122.
[44] This study is specifically concerned with Quebec and the author is well aware that there is a considerable number of francophone Canadians outside of Quebec that would identify by language, region or ethnicity, but not as Québécois.
[45] Cf. OAKES and WARREN, 27.

have to first feel at home in French, the indispensable tool of integration and of access to knowledge, work, culture and citizenship."[46]

Quebec is a country hyperconscious about language. With the disappearance of the authority of the Church and old binaries like the urban-rural divide, still prevalent in the first half of the twentieth century (or the twenty-first century in some regions), language has become the fundamental marker of difference and the most central reference point for identification. Hence far from being only a means of communication, language is a carrier of identity and memory. Moreover it does, in a post-structuralist conception, not represent but construct reality.

In Quebec's case this reality is one of plurality, particularly in its largest city, the Neo-Babel of Montreal, where languages and cultures daily meet and cross, where French and English are in unremitting contact, and where it is "impossible *not* to be involved in the language puzzles that the city constantly throws your way."[47] In his article "*Le français n'est pas en péril*" Italo-Québécois writer Marco Micone remarks on its inhabitants' polyglot sensibility and the polyphony of cultural identities:

> Dans un contexte cosmopolite, l'identité, individuelle ou collective, peut difficilement être traduite par une seule langue. Chez le polyglotte, chacune des langues contribue à la constitution de son identité complexe (dont les langues d'ailleurs ne sont qu'une composante).[48]

Identities can thrive on difference, but they can also be destabilised by it, as pluralism entails challenges and deconstructs the illusion of a nation's distinct and stable core.

Being a minority within the North American context, French-speaking Quebec's need for perpetual self-affirmation involves an ongoing process of re-evaluating its national identity. The province shares this preoccupation with identity with Canada, a nation apparently haunted by the absence of a clear-cut answer to the perennial question, 'What does it mean to be Canadian?' Usually, the country defines itself in overall negative terms, that is, in counter-distinction to its Southern neighbour, whereas francophone Quebecers' essential linguistic difference gives them "a degree of confidence in their cultural identity that Anglophone Canadians lack,"[49] as the French language functions as a kind of "prophylactic against American cultural 'imperialism.'"[50]

---

[46] Qtd. in OAKES and WARREN, 1, 131.
[47] SIMON (2006), xv.
[48] Marco MICONE. "Le français n'est pas en péril." *Le Devoir* 16 Oct. 1999. 19 Aug. 2009 <http://wwwens.uqac.ca/~flabelle/socio/micone.htm>.
[49] OAKES and WARREN, 68.
[50] Andrew HOLMAN and Robert THACKER. "Literary and Popular Culture." In *Canadian Studies in the New Millennium*. Eds. Patrick James and Mark Kasoff. Toronto: U of Toronto P, 2008. 157.

2.2.2. "*Un chiffre que les Montréalais aiment beaucoup*"

In her book *Quebec Identity: The Challenge of Pluralism* Jocelyn Maclure writes:

> This fascination in Quebec with identity issues is not an arcane debate among university academics; it is a live concern that cuts across class, sex, and generational barriers, affecting every citizen who has to live with identity indeterminacy on a daily basis. […] For many observers, the intensity of this self-examination in Quebec evidences a chronic insecurity complex […].[51]

For perhaps as early as 1759 French Canadians started to develop and nourish a long-lasting inferiority complex, since they were dominated by the anglophone minority that asserted its superiority in practically every sector of society for about two centuries. English was the language of success and guaranteed social and economic mobility, so immigrants also tended to adopt English as their language of communication and integration into Canadian society. Consequently Franco-Quebecers were increasingly concerned about *la survivance* of French in the linguistically hostile North American environment; their anxiety was not unjustified if one considers that their natality rate had decreased drastically since the 1960s and that Quebec depended on immigration.[52] Language being an integral, basically indissociable part of their identity, Francophones needed to have the status of French officially recognised and consolidated in Quebec in order to become truly *maîtres chez eux*. For that reason decisive language legislation was introduced in the wake of the Quiet Revolution in Quebec.

On a federal level the Official Languages Act, declaring Canada's English-French bilingualism, was passed under the Trudeau Government in 1969, while the provincial government in Quebec promulgated Bill 63 (*Loi pour promouvoir la langue française au Québec*) in the same year. The latter, however, was perceived to be insufficient and French monolingualism seemed to be the only solution to change the linguistic face of Quebec. In 1974, Bill 22 made French the official language of Quebec, but it was not until 1977 that the most important language law to date was implemented in the province: Bill 101, also known as the "Charter of the French Language."

---

[51] Jocelyn MACLURE. *Quebec Identity: The Challenge of Pluralism*. Montreal: McGill-Queen's UP, 2003. 4.

[52] Cf. Louis-Jacques DORAIS. "Immigration, multiculturalisme et identités canadiennes." In *Perspectives de l'Interculturel*. Ed. Jeannine Blomart and Bernd Krewer. Paris: L'Harmattan, 1994. 147.

The notorious *Loi 101* has brought about the most radical sociolinguistic changes in Quebec, so that French is now used in all spheres of social life again. In its preamble the Charter proclaims:

> [T]he National Assembly of Québec recognizes that Quebecers wish to see the quality and influence of the French language assured, and is resolved therefore to make of French the language of Government and the Law, as well as the normal and everyday language of work, instruction, communication, commerce and business.[53]

Fig. 3

The law prescribes among other things that public signage must be in French only, that companies with more than fifty employees are to conduct their business in French, and that children can only attend an anglophone public school if a parent received primary education in Quebec in English. Although the Charter is still in effect today, some points have been modified and amended, as they were found incompatible with the Canadian Constitution.[54]

Anglophones were mainly outraged by the new legislation, which obliged them, for example, to do business with other Anglophones in French. For them there was an unjust discrepancy between the desire of Quebec's Francophones, who accounted for over 80% of the population, to impose their language and proscribe that of the others. Thus the Charter sparked off a lot of tensions, which were often vented on stop signs (see fig. 4) and the like.

---

[53] GOVERNMENT OF QUEBEC. "The Charter of the French Language – Preamble." 2002. *Office québécois de la langue française*. 21 Aug. 2009 <http://www.olf.gouv.qc.ca/english/charter/preamble.html>.

[54] For example, the article that stipulated that only the French version of legal documents had an official character did not accord with the Constitution and was ruled unlawful. The exclusive use of French in public signage and commercial advertising was likewise considered anti-constitutional by the Supreme Court of Canada, because it was in contradiction with the right of free speech (cf. OAKES and WARREN, 85-88; PÖLL, 108-09. See also Guy ROCHER. "La politique et la loi linguistiques du Québec en 1977." In *Le Français au Québec: 400 ans d'histoire et de vie*. Ed. Michel Plourde. Québec: Fides, 2003. 277).

The number 101 has acquired emblematic power in Quebec and does not solely appear in the form of graffiti. On the occasion of the 350th anniversary of Montreal in 1992, for instance, a big concert attended by 70,000 people was held under the title "*Montréal, ville francophone.*" Its host, Michel Rivard, opened the spectacle by saying that if one counts all the participants (singers, musicians etc), "*on arrive à un chiffre que les Montréalais aiment beaucoup: 101*"[55] – an announcement that earned him enthusiastic cheers from the crowds.

Fig. 4

In Montreal, principal battleground of the French fact in North America and focal point of Québécois culture, the proportion of Francophones is the lowest in the province and dropped to 66% in the Greater Montreal area in the 2006 census.[56] This condition has triggered a high level of insecurity and concern among Francophones about the future of French in the metropolis. However, the measures introduced by the Charter have proved fruitful and both the number of French mother tongue speakers and of allophones who transferred to French has increased within recent years.[57]

Despite its faults, the Charter of the French Language has in any case succeeded in finally making the majority of Quebec's population visible and audible again. It has transformed Quebec into an inclusive society, more accommodating of *les autres* and able to absorb other idioms as well; in fact, it is a sign of the vitality of French in Quebec that it can express various identities today. Eibl also confirms that it is by virtue of Bill 101 that the former French enclave has become a "*société d'accueil.*"[58]

Together with the metamorphosis of Quebec's society as a whole went that of the anglophone population. Although they were a minority, Quebec's Anglos did not

---

[55] In *Montréal, ville francophone.* Dir. Jean-Jacques Sheitoyan. Société Radio-Canada, 1992.
The first performer was Rivard himself, who sang "*Le cœur de ma vie,*" of which the refrain goes: "*C'est une langue de France | Aux accents d'Amérique | [...] C'est la langue de mon cœur | Et le cœur de ma vie | Que jamais elle ne meurt | Que jamais on l'oublie...*"
[56] Cf. Marian SCOTT. "Two Solitudes on Prevalence of French in Montreal: Poll." *Montreal Gazette* 22 June 2009.
[57] Cf. Statistics Canada. "2001 Census: Analysis Series – Profiles of Languages in Canada: English, French and Many Others." *Statcan.ca* 2002. 19 Aug 2009 <http://www12.statcan.ca/english/census01/Products/Analytic/companion/lang/pdf/96F0030XIE2001005.pdf>. 10.
[58] Doris EIBL. *Romaneske Un-Heimlichkeiten im Spannungsfeld von Postmoderne und "Ecriture au féminin."* Dissertation, University of Innsbruck, 1999. 22.

perceive themselves as one, as they dominated almost all of the province until about fifty years ago. Today one can speak of a virtual role reversal; but Anglo-Quebecers, substantially reduced in both numbers and influence, seem to have accepted their minority status and even Bill 101: "Every now and then something comes up related to Bill 101, but the communities seem to be getting along for the most part. Don't ask us if we support Bill 101, but we've learned to live with it. We're at a happy medium,"[59] says Robert Donnelly, president of the Anglo Quebec Community Groups network.

2.3. Literary Voices

> Love consists in this,
> that two solitudes protect,
> and touch, and greet each other.
> - Rainer Maria Rilke[60] -

Canadian literary history is not exactly replete with reflections about the English-French dynamic, but although anglophone and francophone literatures in Canada have developed along fairly independent trajectories and led largely parallel lives, neither side failed to express the country's bicultural reality. Literature, frequently invoked as a mirror of society, was often used, or abused, for political purposes and interspersed with moral messages, which ranged from humorous as in *Une partie de campagne* (first performed in 1857) – a comic warning against the adoption of English speech by dramatist Pierre Petitclair – to vitriolic as in *Poignet d'acier* (1863). The latter is a work by Henri-Emile Chevalier, who wrote several political romances arguing for revenge; in the above mentioned novel, for instance, a deathbed utterance urges, *"Vivez pour arracher le Canada à l'odieuse tyrannie anglaise."*[61] Yet, from early on stories also portrayed cross-cultural relationships, like that of a young French Canadian and an English officer in *Antoinette; or, Secret Marrying and Secret Sorrowing* (1864), for example.

---

[59] Qtd. in Hubert BAUCH. "French-English Relations in Quebec at a 'Happy Medium.'" *Montreal Gazette* 21 June 2009.
[60] Qtd. in Hugh MACLENNAN. *Two Solitudes*. 1945. Toronto: General Paperbacks, 1991. n.p.
[61] Qtd. in W.H. NEW. *A History of Canadian Literature*. Montreal: McGill-Queen's UP, 2001. 67.

In his *History of Canadian Literature* W.H. New[62] agrees that there was literary communication between anglophone and francophone Canada in the nineteenth century. However, he observes that

> [...] the two versions of nationhood spilled over into literary *topoi*; Quebec tales of martyrdom and the *maudits anglais* countered Ontario tales of quaint habitant, sophisticated Protestant and corrupt Catholic. Prejudices on both sides fed the tales; the mistake was to accept the *topoi* of tale-telling for historical fact.[63]

This dichotomy is very well captured in the paradigmatic work on that subject, namely Hugh MacLennan's *Two Solitudes* (1945). The novel's title has since entered the Canadian collective consciousness and is still widely used to describe the situation of separation and non-dialogue between the anglophone and francophone communities.

In Quebec the onset of the Quiet Revolution and subsequent tensions gave rise to an immense imaginative fertility; indeed the precarious cultural, linguistic and political situation seemed to unleash the nation's creative potential. All literary genres have functioned as productive arenas for debates on language and identity with sometimes more and sometimes less innovative meditations on the English-French binarism. Some scholars claim that the two linguistic camps "rarely meet or cross over in literature, film, or theatre" and that they have not really tried to engage one another.[64] However, this statement hardly paints an accurate picture, especially not as far as theatre is concerned, because it is there that one can witness a considerable number of instances of very original cultural and linguistic *métissage*, as in the plays of Michel Tremblay, David Fennario and others. Examples include a bilingual production of *Romeo & Juliette* (with English being spoken by the Montagues and a francophone Capulet family), *L'homme invisible* (the protagonist is incarnated by two actors, one francophone, the other anglophone) and Montreal's theatre group Theatre 1774, which works simultaneously in both languages for purely artistic rather than political reasons.[65]

---

[62] It is interesting to note that, apart from New's important work, literary histories that treat both English- and French-Canadian literature have often come from outside of Canada. Two notable contributions were made by German-speaking academia: *Kanadische Literaturgeschichte* (2005, edited by Konrad Groß, Wolfgang Klooß and Reingard M. Nischik) and *History of Literature in Canada: English-Canadian and French-Canadian* (2008, edited by Reingard M. Nischik).

[63] NEW, 86.

[64] HOLMAN and THACKER, 154.

[65] Cf. Philip SPENSLEY. "Franglo théâtre – esthétique et politique: Reaching Out to a Bilingual Audience, ou quoi ?" In *Cultural Identities in Canadian Literature*. Ed. Bénédicte Mauguière. NY: Lang, 1998. 163, 166.

A notable verse piece that takes up the language controversy is Michèle Lalonde's *Speak White*, first recited at the *Nuit de la poésie* in Montreal in 1970 and later published in *Défense et illustration de la langue québécoise*. In her overtly political poem Lalonde tries to defend the French language and the 'black world' of the francophone population, whom she contrasts in an ironic tone with those who are superior, since they 'speak white' – meaning English. About two decades later Marco Micone published a well-known retort, *Speak What*, in which he points to the changed position of the former *"peuple-concierge"* and draws attention to the fact that the nation's duality has given way to plurality as caused by immigration.[66] Micone is one of the so-called neo-Québécois writers like Dany Laferrière, Ying Chen and Emile Ollivier, who have substituted the black-and-white picture of French-English antagonism with a new colourful mix and refreshing diversity.

After the politically charged 1960s and 70s one can discern a kind of conviviality in Quebec literature with an important impetus coming from the immigrant population. The redefinition of paradigms since the 1980s manifests itself among other things in creative and innovative phenomena like code-switching or a hybrid use of language (e.g. *Voice-Over* by Carole Corbeil, 1992), which led some scholars to remark that Quebec can boast of a "distinct cultural production that is the envy of Anglophone Canada."[67] Exchange is vital for a culture in order to flourish and to remain vibrant; according to Nadine Ltaif, Quebec literature owes its originality to the contact between English and French: *"L'originalité de [l]a création littéraire québécoise résulte du métissage français-anglais. La création littéraire est au carrefour des langues, le point de rencontre des cultures."*[68] This study will now investigate how this originality reveals itself in contemporary literature of Montreal and how the theme of the two solitudes is approached in fiction of the post-Bill 101 and post-referenda period.

---

[66] Cf. Ursula MATHIS. "'Speak What'?: Observations à propos de la littérature immigrée au Québec." *Neue Romania* 18 (1997): 25. For an in-depth discussion of Québécois poetry see Ursula MATHIS. "La poésie québécoise: un bilan." In *Etudes québécoises: bilan et perspectives.* Ed. Hans-Josef Niederehe. Tübingen: Niemeyer, 1996. 131-51.
[67] OAKES and WARREN, 73.
[68] Nadine LTAIF. "Ecrire pour vivre l'échange entre les langues." In *Literary Pluralities.* Ed. Christl Verduyn. Peterborough: Broadview Press, 1998. 82.

3. Methodological Considerations and Contextualisation

> The French and the English don't communicate enough in Quebec. It's as if [they] spoke two completely different languages.[69]

Jokes are one example of creative output springing from the linguistically and culturally charged situation in Quebec. While political tensions between Francophones/Anglophones and Quebec/Canada are less fraught today than they were from the 1960s to mid-90s, a time which saw such events as the Quiet Revolution, the FLQ crisis and the two referenda, old and new sources of friction remain numerous. With a myriad of political, sociological, historical, linguistic and even philosophical studies having been devoted to the English-French dichotomy in Quebec, the discourse seems exhausted. Yet, some scholars bemoan the absence of a cultural discussion; in his book, *Impossible Nation*, inspired by events surrounding the 1995 referendum, Ray Conlogue wonders, "Why is this, considering that almost everybody in Canada agrees that the problem is essentially cultural?"[70] Responding to Conlogue's concern, the present study seeks to examine the treatment of anglophone-francophone interactions in contemporary Montreal literature.

It is virtually impossible to dissociate literature from society; Gilles Marcotte goes as far as to declare that "*toute œuvre littéraire [...] parle de la société, fait parler la société ou [...] la société parle en elle.*"[71] How does literature make present-day society 'speak,' now that the most turbulent times of Québécois history appear to have calmed down, and that the major literary voices of that era – Gabrielle Roy, Hubert Aquin and Mordecai Richler, to name just a few – have largely passed on? As an exemplary and comparative analysis, this study uses selected works by Monique Proulx and Neil Bissoondath as illustrations of cultural phenomena. Yet, the present analysis in no way intends to equate literary representations with reality,[72] but it ex-

---

[69] Rick BLUE. "No Shortage of Jokes About Anglos." *Montreal Gazette* 26 March 2009.
[70] Ray CONLOGUE. *Impossible Nation: The Longing for Homeland in Canada and Quebec*. Stratford: The Mercury Press, 1996. 8.
[71] Qtd. in Noémi SHIRINIAN. *La mosaïque comme métaphore de l'autre dans* Les Aurores montréales *de Monique Proulx*. M.A. thesis, Queen's University Kingston, 2001. 2 Sept. 2009 <http://www.collectionscanada.gc.ca/obj/s4/f2/dsk3/ftp04/MQ59402.pdf>. 26.
[72] John Gibson suggests that "literature's relation to the world is better understood as *foundational* rather than representational, consisting in literature's ability to bring before us narratives that hold

plores how texts of fiction treat certain themes concerning the anglophone-francophone duality. The procedure is comparative, as similarities and differences in content, form and structure are highlighted, while the English-French discourse is at the same time being critically investigated. Moreover, given that the subject is extremely vast and widely ramified, the approach cannot but be selective. It is the aim of this chapter to explain the reasons behind the decisions that had to be taken. Answers are thus provided to the question why this study scrutinises Montreal literature and these specific works of narrative fiction by Proulx and Bissoondath in particular and at the present time.

3.1. Montreal – A Doubly Postcolonial City

> Piège. La cité écartée à tout fendre. En son centre, gémir. S'être prise. Dorénavant en son double fond de mémoire, son centre double de ville double: araignée du soir, araignée du matin. De chagrin. Plusieurs verbes avant que d'être prise au dépourvu. D'avoir perdu son temps.
>
> A trap. The city's soul divided, clove in two. In its middle, moans. Having been caught. Henceforth in its double depths of memory, the double centre of a double city, there's east and west and between the twain. And pain. Several verbs before being caught short. For having taken leave of our tenses.
>
> - Nicole Brossard[73] -

By talking of Montreal's "*double fond de mémoire*" ("double depths of memory"), Brossard is referring to the persistent legacies of French and British colonisation in Quebec. Being historically enshrined in the city, the language dichotomy is, moreover, a geographical issue. Nevertheless, this study neither includes an isolated analysis of setting per se nor will it enlarge in detail upon space theories as advanced by intellectuals such as Heidegger, Benjamin, Lefebvre, de Certeau, Foucault or Bourdieu. However, since the problem manifests itself most perceptibly in Montreal, an analysis

---

in place and give structure to our understanding of large expanses of cultural reality" (John GIBSON. *Fiction and the Weave of Life*. Oxford: Oxford UP, 2007. 10).

[73] English translation by Patricia Claxton, cited in SIMON (2006), 149-50.

of anglophone-francophone interactions is inseparable from its setting, as will be discussed in the following.

Writers and scholars have used various attributes to describe Quebec's economic and cultural metropolis. The dual or double city – denominations under which Montreal is frequently summoned – is the world's second largest francophone city after Paris; and where bilingualism once meant Francophones speaking English, it now means Anglophones (and Allophones) speaking French. Furthermore, having undergone double colonisation, Montreal is also a postcolonial city, which is apparent in its fragmented character.[74] Although one should be wary of such simplistic formulations, Montreal is generally portrayed as a city spatially divided into two parts: a francophone East and an anglophone West, separated by the Saint-Laurent Boulevard, more commonly known as "The Main." The idea of Montreal's inherent biculturalism has been replaced by a more accurate understanding of the agglomeration of diverse ethnic and linguistic groupings, so that one is perfectly justified in calling Montreal a cosmopolitan city. Quebec's largest metropolis has truly developed into an international city that has learned within the last century to deal with globalisation and mass migration. Montreal is thus also a postmodern city[75] capable of profoundly disconcerting newcomers with its Babelian disorder, which may have induced the writer Régine Robin to call Montreal a *"[v]ille schizophrène."*[76] Doris Sommer agrees that the "unsettled poignancy of too many languages and not enough of one makes Montreal an *unheimlich* home."[77]

Montreal is French-speaking, but not a French city. Instead, it is unquestionably a North American city – though probably the most European one[78] – that draws heavily on both its *américanité* and *francité*. In this it remains isolated in the North American context, thus being an island in more than just the literal geographic

---

[74] Montreal is, moreover, a city that wears its history on its sleeve, that is to say that its fragmentation and different influences are also discernible in its architecture.
[75] Edwards and Ivison describe the city as "the site par excellence in the elaboration of the postmodern subject, as its constantly reconstructed streets and alleys, its forever changing cafés and restaurants, represent a fragmented mental map that reflects a decentred sense of self" (Justin D. EDWARDS and Douglas IVISON. "Epilogue." In *Downtown Canada: Writing Canadian Cities.* Eds. Justin D. Edwards and Douglas Ivison. Toronto: U of Toronto P, 2005. 204).
[76] Régine ROBIN. *La québécoite*. Montréal: Editions Québec, 1983. 78.
[77] Doris SOMMER. Ed. *Bilingual Games: Some Literary Investigations.* NY: Palgrave Macmillan, 2003. 14.
[78] Cf. DUFRESNE, 13. See also LINTEAU, 573.

sense.[79] Quebec's largest city is also different from the rest of the province, which is rather homogenous in comparison, as there the proportion of Francophones comes close to a hundred per cent in some regions, whereas in the Montreal area Anglophones and Allophones concentrate. Additionally, one should stress Montreal's urban quality here. Michel de Certeau, for example, talks about a city's "texturology in which extremes coincide,"[80] while Walter Benjamin conceives of the (post-) modern metropolis as a labyrinth and is fascinated by the constant flux of the urban milieu where the "stamp of the definitive is avoided."[81]

Despite being an island and therefore physically somewhat shut off, Montreal has managed to welcome a highly diversified population into its territory. The city's palimpsest of histories, memories and languages has created very complex and multivalent constructions of cultural identity. Homi Bhabha argues that all forms of culture are essentially hybrid and that it is in the 'in-between' spaces that the most innovative and creative cultural productions emerge.[82] Consequently, the co-existence of and contact between a multitude of different people may be assumed to have added significantly to Montreal's imaginative potential. Sherry Simon declares that "[l]anguages, like ideas, take on density when they touch,"[83] which is another aspect that makes the multilingual city unique. In her book, *Translating Montreal: Episodes in the Life of a Divided City*, Simon further asks what Montreal would be without the language difference and concedes that this is a provocative question, since to eclipse

---

[79] In an interview Monique Proulx says the following about Montreal's ambiguous place: "*Montréal est une île. L'océan nous rappelle l'immensité du continent et, en même temps, notre isolement. [...] On se sent comme faisant partie de l'Amérique du Nord, mais on n'est pas Américains... C'est pas nous... Il y a des convergences et des divergences entre le Québec et la France, le Québec et l'Amérique, le Québec et le Canada anglophone. [...] Nous sommes une sorte de point de jonction entre tous. [...]C'est intimement lié à notre passé: origine française, promiscuité anglophone, culture américaine, développement d'une réalité très pointue et très actuelle au Québec même. C'est une situation privilégiée, même si elle est très inconfortable.*" (qtd. in "Malgré nous, nous transportons le Québec sur nos épaules." *Synopsis*. 2000. 2 Sept. 2009 <http://declic.com/synopsis/ monique.htm>).

[80] He speaks of "extremes of ambition and degradation, brutal oppositions of races and styles, contrasts between yesterday's buildings [...] and today's urban irruptions [...]." Michel DE CERTEAU. "Walking in the City." In *The Cultural Studies Reader*. Ed. Simon During. London: Routledge, 1994. 152.

[81] Qtd. in Simon PARKER. *Urban Theory and the Urban Experience: Encountering the City*. London: Routledge, 2004. 16, 18.

[82] Cf. Homi K. BHABHA. *The Location of Culture*. London: Routledge, 1994. 1-2.

[83] SIMON (2006), 219.

the language difference would be to eliminate "the very substance of Montreal's cultural history."[84]

The language-conscious city thus offers an unequalled setting and frame to investigate exchanges between Quebec's two major linguistic communities. It is there that the francophone majority remains fragile and that the English language is at its most vital. In fact, it is possible in Montreal to live one's life entirely in English without ever bothering to adequately speak (or learn) the language of the majority,[85] like the respective protagonists in Bissoondath's *Doing the Heart Good* and "Les aurores montréales," the eponymous story of Proulx's short story collection, for instance.

In the course of the twentieth century Montreal went through a series of profound transformations. Yet, with the turn of the century the metropolis has changed again and new categories of identity are surfacing in the once-divided city. Sherry Simon speaks of a "new Montreal of increasingly relaxed social interactions," which has witnessed since the late 1990s the emergence of the "'new' Anglo- or Franco-Montrealer, the bilingual, often trilingual, individual who navigates the entire city with ease."[86] Might it be now, in a Montreal that is becoming more and more diverse and multilingual, that the image of the two solitudes has finally lost its validity? The next section introduces two authors presently living and writing in Quebec who broach the subject of the two solitudes in contemporary Montreal.

3.2. Two Contemporary Spokespersons and Their Oeuvre

In order to paint a more complete picture of Montreal's English-French duality, fiction by writers from both sides of the linguistic divide is explored in detail in the present study. The francophone perspective shall be represented by Monique Proulx, a Quebec writer of novels, short stories and screenplays, who is also well and widely received in English Canada. Another member of Quebec's intellectual elite, Neil Bis-

---

[84] SIMON (2006), 206.
[85] The same point is made by Montreal writer Gail Scott, who adds, "With ignorance, I'm sorry to say, sometimes goes contempt" (Gail SCOTT. "My Montréal: Notes of an Anglo-Québécois Writer." *Brick* 59 (Spring 1998): 5).
[86] SIMON (2006), 8, 10. Montreal has the highest rate of trilingualism in Canada, with 22.2% on the island of Montreal knowing at least three languages according to the 2001 census (cf. OAKES and WARREN, 145).

soondath is studied for his articulation of what can be seen as a distinctly anglophone angle.

Born within a couple of years of each other in the early 1950s, Proulx and Bissoondath are today prominent representatives of Quebec's cultural and literary scene, reaching a large audience within and beyond the province. Proulx, a Francophone *de souche*, was born in Quebec City and settled in Montreal in 1984, whereas Canada has been Bissoondath's chosen home ever since he emigrated from Trinidad at the age of eighteen. Although they approach disparate subject matters for the most part, both authors are generally eager to afford their characters moments of happiness and human warmth despite their hardships. In Proulx's work, for instance, there is often a particular *joie de vivre*; the author herself states in an interview, "*Je ne suis pas une jovialiste, mais je trouve qu'on sous-estime la vie*," and she concludes, "*La vie est bonne pour moi.*"[87] Humour, especially in the form of irony, in fact characterises much of her writing, giving a positive note even to gloomy themes such as poverty, alcoholism, (trans-)sexuality, racism and others.

In 1983 Proulx[88] published her first book, a short story collection entitled *Sans cœur et sans reproche*; it was followed by two novels: *Le Sexe des étoiles* (1987), which was turned into a critically and commercially successful film, and *Homme invisible à la fenêtre* (1993). A second short story collection was published in 1996 under the title *Les Aurores montréales*, which embodies a literary microcosm of a multifaceted Montreal. After *Le Cœur est un muscle involontaire* (2002) Proulx abandoned the city as her preferred setting and turned to nature in her most recent novel *Champagne* (2008).

The anglophone presence in Montreal features only sporadically in her work, as in the form of individual characters like Julius Einhorne in *Homme invisible à la fenêtre*, for example.[89] It may surprise readers that Anglophones are sometimes conspicuously absent from Proulx's novels, given that the author is a long-term resident

---

[87] Christian DESMEULES. "Entretien – La vraie nature de Monique Proulx." *Le Devoir* 15/16 March 2008.

[88] For the following see also: Margaret COOK. "Proulx, Monique." In *Encyclopedia of Literature in Canada*. Ed. W.H. New. Toronto: U of Toronto P, 2002. 903.

[89] The novel in question contains several instances of heterolingualism, a term introduced by Rainier Grutman to denote multilingual elements in a literary work (cf. Rainier GRUTMAN. *Des langues qui résonnent: L'hétérolinguisme au XIXe siècle québécois*. Saint-Laurent: Fides, 1997. 11). Heterolinguistic passages spoken by the anglophone Julius Einhorne include: "[...] c'est moi qui vendrai les tickets juste à la porte devant chez vous, can you see it, you working and me collecting the money devant une file longue de very well-dressed people" (Monique PROULX. *Homme invisible à la fenêtre*. Québec: Boréal/Seuil, 1993. 99-100).

of Montreal and an astute observer of her environment. In *Le Cœur est un muscle involontaire* the city's major language groups are represented (e.g. one of the main characters is a Francophone of Italian and Mohawk origin, who spends most of his time together with the protagonist at Therios' Greek restaurant) with the noticeable exception of Anglo-Montrealers. Apart from the occasional cyber jargon and swearing in English, the only linguistic hint that the story is set in Montreal is given by a taxi driver, who replies to the protagonist's French directions – interestingly – by saying, "Yes, Madame."[90]

For the purpose of this study, *Les Aurores montréales* constitutes the main object of investigation on the francophone side. The collection of twenty-seven short stories draws a realistic portrait of Montreal spanning approximately the decade of the 1990s, during which Quebec secession was a burning issue before and after the 1995 referendum. As Proulx sets all of the stories in Montreal, she makes it impossible for herself not to address francophone-anglophone interactions. These figure in one way or the other in a considerable number of the stories, predominantly so in the title piece "Les aurores montréales," "Oui or no" and *"Blanc,"* which will be looked into in special detail.

The anglophone writer Neil Bissoondath[91] has published an impressive range of fiction, but it is his work of non-fiction – *Selling Illusions: The Cult of Multiculturalism in Canada* (1994, revised 2002) – that has caused the greatest furore in Canada. In this most controversial and best-selling book by Bissoondath he forwards a vehement critique of Canadian multicultural policy, which, he argues, is ghettoising the nation rather than promoting a common sense of belonging. His novels and short stories also explore themes of belonging, uprootedness and cultural alienation. Faced with exile, his characters, usually immigrants, are caught between confronting their respective pasts and forging a new sense of identity for themselves.

His first book, a short story collection called *Digging Up the Mountains*, appeared in 1985 and was followed by a further collection of short stories *On the Eve of Uncertain Tomorrows* (1990), which deals with the plight of exiles and their pursuit

---

[90] Monique PROULX. *Le cœur est un muscle involontaire*. Montréal: Boréal, 2002. 318. It is difficult to ascertain why Proulx makes the taxi driver reply in English, but perhaps it just shows that in a truly multilingual place people are simply prone to arbitrary code-switching.
[91] Cf. Daniel COLEMAN. "Bissoondath, Neil." In *Encyclopedia of Literature in Canada*. Ed. W.H. New. Toronto: U of Toronto P, 2002. 122. See also: Brian John BUSBY. "Bissoondath, Neil Devindra." *The Canadian Encyclopedia*. 2009. Historica Foundation of Canada. 4 Sept. 2009 <http://www.thecanadianencyclopedia.com/index.cfm?PgNm=TCE&Params=A1ARTA0010093>.

of the 'Canadian Dream,' which is often impeded by the characters' feeling that they are overcome by a "fearful impotence."[92] Bissoondath published three novels – *A Casual Brutality* (1988), *The Innocence of Age* (1992) and *The Worlds Within Her* (1998) – before opting for a departure from his preferred themes in *Doing the Heart Good* in 2002. He returns to themes such as racism and political unrest in *The Unyielding Clamour of the Night* (2005), succeeded three years later by another novel, *The Soul of All Great Designs*, and a novella in 2009.

Doing the Heart Good forms the focus of the present study and is an atypical work within Bissoondath's œuvre. Its main characters are neither immigrants nor are they mired in a search for identity.[93] The protagonist and first-person narrator is a seventy-five-year-old anglophone Montrealer who re-evaluates his life after having lost his house and possessions to an arsonist, and forced to live in his daughter's household. The centrality of language to life in Montreal is expressed in the following brief plot summary:

> Alistair Mackenzie has lived his life in a francophone society refusing to speak a word of French. He must now live with his bilingual (anglophone) daughter, her bilingual (francophone) husband, and their six-year-old son, who understands English but speaks only French.[94]

In Mackenzie's episodic first-person narrative there is a whole menagerie of characters, but reading the novel specifically with regard to the language divide, the present analysis concentrates on the protagonist's conflicts with his grandson François, his son-in-law Jacques and his neighbour Tremblay. These conflicts are not dramatised from the beginning to the end but subtly developed throughout the novel and deserve closer attention, because they appear central to the story.

---

[92] Neil BISSOONDATH. "On the Eve of Uncertain Tomorrows." In *Multiculturalism and Immigration in Canada: An Introductory Reader*. Ed. Elspeth Cameron. Toronto: Canadian Scholars' Press, 2004. 330.
[93] The author himself alleges that there is "no question of identity" in this novel (qtd. in Celia SANKAR. "Author of His Own Destiny." *Américas* 53 (July 2001): 51). However, this seems to be an overstatement considering that the story consists of the protagonist's retrospective look at his own existence.
[94] SANKAR, 51.

3.3. Some Reflections on Genre

The fact that this study draws on different genres and approaches to deal with the topic of the two solitudes in present-day Montreal should not be regarded as complicating but rather as enriching the discussion. Since problems often arise from failing to see the other point of view, varied perspectives are crucial. Yet, similarities between Bissoondath's novel and Proulx's short story collection – as those between Montreal's two biggest language communities – far outweigh the differences between them. Besides, Bissoondath points out that *Doing the Heart Good* started out as a short story, but as the main character came to him and refused to leave, the story developed into a book about "the same character, relating his life in a series of stories but also linking them all by means of a present tense that gives a kind of unity to the entire thing." The author moreover says that he considers the final form as "a blend of the short story and the novel."[95]

In her discussion of the French-Canadian short story in *History of Literature in Canada* (2008), Eibl likewise asserts that the generic boundaries of the novel and the various forms of short prose are fluid. This makes generic classification sometimes quite difficult; Jacques Ferron, for example, published novels which were also labelled "*grands contes*." Eibl elaborates furthermore:

> The parallels in the development of the Quebec novel and short prose, which are especially prominent on the content level, can be explained by the fact that the majority of the short stories that entered the literary canon had been written by novelists.[96]

As for the English-Canadian short story, Nischik also attributes its continuing success and the vitality of the genre to the fact that "major Canadian writers have almost without exception devoted considerable effort to the form"[97] to the point that one critic described the contemporary Canadian short story as "the literary equivalent of a national display of fireworks."[98]

---

[95] Qtd. in Laurie KRUK. "'All Voices Belong to Me' – An Interview with Neil Bissoondath." *Canadian Literature* 180 (Spring 2004): 62-63.

[96] Doris G. EIBL. "The French-Canadian Short Story." In *History of Literature in Canada: English-Canadian and French-Canadian*. Ed. Reingard M. Nischik. Rochester: Camden House, 2008. 269. See also page 264, 268.

[97] Reingard M. NISCHIK. "The Canadian Short Story: Status, Criticism, Historical Survey." In *The Canadian Short Story: Interpretations*. Ed. Reingard M. Nischik. Rochester: Camden House, 2007. 1.

[98] Qtd. in Reingard M. NISCHIK. "The English-Canadian Short Story since 1967: Between (Post)Modernism and (Neo)Realism." In *History of Literature in Canada: English-Canadian and French-Canadian*. Ed. Reingard M. Nischik. Rochester: Camden House, 2008. 333.

While both pieces are works of narrative fiction, *Doing the Heart Good* and *Les Aurores montréales* still belong to different genres. Short prose differs from long prose fiction not only in length, but also in structure and style, usually containing only a limited number of characters and rarely a shift of narrative voice. Apart from that, the short story's possibilities to develop setting, characters and action are normally restricted, but the genre allows for its limitations to be compensated by leaving gaps and creating ambiguities through omissions. Misao Dean submits the following modern-day definition of the short story:

> The fast pace of "modern" life and the demand of readers for intense experiences seemed to suggest a correspondingly short and intense prose form [...]: a story unified in place, action and time, whose dramatization of a revelatory and emotionally intense moment manages to suggest the outcome of a complete "life story" in a concentrated form.[99]

In their introduction to *A la carte: Le roman québécois (2000-2005)* the editors argue that "*le genre romanesque [...] constitue un terrain privilégié pour apprécier les changements survenus dans une littérature en rapport avec la société qui l'a vue naître, voire qui lui a donné le jour;*" and they continue by asserting that it is "*plus apte sans doute que tout autre genre à représenter un « certain état » de la littérature et de la société qui lui est contemporaine.*"[100] However, short prose is equally suited to convey the state of contemporary Quebec society, as Proulx's stories in *Les Aurores montréales* do, combining to make up a vivid portrait of a diverse, multiethnic, ever-changing Montreal at the close of the twentieth century. In his study of the genre Jean-Pierre Boucher writes about the short story collection:

> Le recueil de nouvelles permet [au nouvelliste] de traduire sa perception fragmentaire d'un monde en perpétuel changement, lui permet surtout de rendre compte des limites, de l'impossibilité ou du refus d'une vision du monde unifiée, synthétique. Éclatement, relativité, mouvement, morcellement, discontinuité, instabilité, rupture, questionnement, inquiétude, incertitude, voilà autant d'aspects de la sensibilité contemporaine que le recueil exprime peut-être mieux qu'un roman suivi. Au monolithe, on préfère le fragment.[101]

As one cannot render such a thing as the essence of a city, a book composed of literary fragments in the form of short stories correlates perhaps most adequately to a very complex Montreal that is itself highly fragmented.

The English-Canadian short story is a relatively young literary phenomenon. As a national genre it began to coalesce in the 1890s, but fully emerged in the 1920s dur-

---

[99] Qtd. in NISCHIK (2007), 5-6.
[100] Gilles DUPUIS and Klaus-Dieter ERTLER. "Introduction." In *A la carte: Le roman québécois (2000-2005)*. Eds. Gilles Dupuis and Klaus-Dieter Ertler. Frankfurt, Wien: Lang, 2007. 12.
[101] Qtd. in SHIRINIAN, 56.

ing modernism, experiencing its first heyday in the 1960s. In French Canada, the genre followed a different evolution. Short pieces were produced as early as the 1830s, though it is in the 1860s with the Abbé Henri-Raymond Casgrain that one really speaks of recognisable short fiction.[102] French-Canadian short stories (in English translation) were included for the first time in the *Canadian Short Stories* anthology in 1958. In the introduction the editor explains:

> There have been good reasons for restricting Canadian anthologies to writing in one language, and there is no sense pretending that even today there is a consistent or vital connexion between the literatures of French and English Canada. But in the past few years some short stories from French Canada […] have been published or broadcast in translation, and it seemed worth recognizing this important, if hesitant, meeting of the two cultures by reprinting three of those stories here.[103]

Regarding the contrasts between short-story writing in English and French Canada, Nischik further states that in the latter the short story is not a major literary form, although developments in the 1980s and 1990s led critics to speak of "the golden age of short prose" in Quebec; yet, it remains a *"genre plutôt pour* happy few."[104] Eibl suggests that the hesitant reception by francophone audiences is not only due to the fact that the short story in Quebec has always been overshadowed by the novel, but also because of often difficult aesthetics concentrating on form.[105]

As far as recent developments are concerned, there seems to be more and more blending between the genres. Mutual influences are evident, for example, in the striving for thematic and/or structural unity in short-story volumes. This endeavour has probably less to do "with literary theoretical considerations than with the dynamics of the book market, which prefer[s] the coherent narration of the novel,"[106] according to Eibl. Genre hybridity is in fact typical of the last two decades of the twentieth cen-

---

[102] Cf. NISCHIK (2007), 1, 3. See also Reingard M. NISCHIK. "The Modernist English-Canadian Short Story." In *History of Literature in Canada: English-Canadian and French-Canadian*. Ed. Reingard M. Nischik. Rochester: Camden House, 2008. 194. Of course, English-Canadian short narratives also existed in the early nineteenth century, but they were myths and sketches more than stories (cf. Robert Thacker. "Short Fiction." In *The Cambridge Companion to Canadian Literature*. Ed. Eva-Marie Kröller. Cambridge: Cambridge UP, 2004. 179).
[103] Qtd. in NISCHIK (2007), 17.
[104] Qtd. in NISCHIK (2007), 18. Moreover, she writes that "the less established French-Canadian *conte* is more open to narrative experimentation than the English-Canadian short story" (ibid).
[105] Cf. Doris G. EIBL. "The French-Canadian Short Prose Narrative." In *History of Literature in Canada: English-Canadian and French-Canadian*. Ed. Reingard M. Nischik. Rochester: Camden House, 2008. 454-55.
[106] EIBL. "The French-Canadian Short Prose Narrative." (2008), 452. See also page 453 for the following.

tury. In addition, many texts feature intertextual references; several of Proulx's stories are a case in point.

3.4. Circumstantial History of the Works Discussed

Both Proulx and Bissoondath are popular with francophone and anglophone readerships. A reviewer of the English translation of *Les Aurores montréales*, for instance, concludes, "Finishing this book, the reader is convinced Monique Proulx is yet another reason why Canada would be infinitely poorer without Quebec."[107] As for *Doing the Heart Good*, it won – tellingly so – the Hugh MacLennan Award for the best English book written in Quebec in 2002.[108] The two authors have been nominated for various awards and prizes, such as the prestigious Governor General's Literary Award (Bissoondath was shortlisted in 1999, Proulx in 2002 and 2008), which honours writers in French and English in different categories including translation.

Apart from writing prize-winning literature, both authors have seen their work published in translation. With the exception of her first book, all of Proulx's fiction has been translated into English and mostly published within a year of the original (excluding her latest novel, a translation of which has not yet appeared), while Lori Saint-Martin and Paul Gagné were awarded the Translation Prize by the Quebec Writers' Federation in 2004 for *Un baume pour le cœur*, the French version of *Doing the Heart Good*. In fact, one can speak nowadays of an "almost systematic translation of Montreal writers in both directions,"[109] which also leads to innovative translation practices such as self-translation. A well-known example of literary self-translation is offered by the Canadian writer Nancy Huston, a bilingual anglophone author now living in France, who writes primarily in French, but who has translated the better part of her work into her mother tongue. Another bilingual writer who publishes books in both French and English, and who occasionally translates her own work, is Montreal-born Nathalie Stephens.

---

[107] Maureen GARVIE. "*Aurora Montrealis* by Monique Proulx." *Quill & Quire* Dec. 1997. St. Joseph Media Inc. 4 Sept. 2009 <http://www.quillandquire.com/reviews/review.cfm?review_id=270>.
[108] Cf. Nicholas DINKA. "Hard Questions: Neil Bissoondath Takes on a Controversial Subject in His Timely New Novel." *Quill & Quire* Sept. 2005. St. Joseph Media Inc. 4 Sept. 2009 <http://www.quillandquire.com/authors/profile.cfm?article_id=6856>.
[109] SIMON (2006), 207.

Proulx and Bissoondath take part in Quebec's vibrant literary culture,[110] which can pride itself on many unique and original creative productions, which are not least due to the conflict between languages that can be both divisive and fruitful. Generally, Anglo-Quebec authors have more often shown themselves to be affected by the stimulus coming from this tension between languages and cultures in Montreal, whereas a considerable number of francophone writers have taken up the experience of a Québécois in Paris and thus engaged in a fictional escape to their former *mère-patrie*. Indeed, Paris still seems to hover like a super-ego over some Franco-Québécois. In *Downtown Canada*, which seeks to deconstruct Canadian literature's long obsession with wilderness, the authors also affirm that "the metropolitan self in Canadian narratives has often been located elsewhere, in New York or London or Paris."[111]

Books released within the last ten to fifteen years by contemporary authors that discuss the issue of the two solitudes are extremely scarce. In 2004, for instance, Gisèle Villeneuve published *Visiting Elizabeth*, in which the bilingual author develops a hybrid language, as the francophone protagonist begins to incarnate her deceased English-speaking friend.[112] But similar to other recently published books such as Michel Basilières' gothic novel *Black Bird*, which is set during the October Crisis, *Visiting Elizabeth* does not deal with contemporary Montreal society, as the story unfolds in the riotous 1960s. Exceptions like *Doing the Heart Good* that do scrutinise anglophone-francophone interactions in today's Montreal are few and far between, and include, for example, Jeffrey Moore's *Prisoner in a Red-Rose Chain* (1999), written in English and set in his hometown Montreal. In an interview Moore explains his fascination with the city and its hybridity: "*Parce que c'est une des plus belles villes d'Amérique du Nord. J'aime la notion de deux cultures et faire partie d'une minorité: je me sens moins comme un mouton, moins anonyme et conformiste.*"[113]

---

[110] Quebec's publishing industry has expanded significantly since the second half of the twentieth century. Victor Lévy-Beaulieu chartered its growth during his lifetime: "4 novels in 1948, some 40 in 1978, about 400 in 1998, and 540 in 2000" (John DICKINSON and Brian YOUNG. *A Short History of Quebec*. 4th ed. Montreal: McGill-Queen's UP, 2008. 369).

[111] EDWARDS and IVISON, 199. In this respect it is important to remember that Bissoondath offers the perspective of an anglophone writer who has no European migration background.

[112] As a result, the novel as a whole is only accessible to a bilingual readership; consider for example: "[..] je pense, is Elizabeth the English pendant to la discrétion de maman, must I now discover la vie in the silences between the words of two languages [...]" (Gisèle VILLENEUVE. *Visiting Elizabeth*. Montreal: XYZ Publishing, 2004. 75).

[113] Qtd. in N. KAMALA. "Traduire la diversité: un roman montréalais en anglais." *Synergies Inde* 3 (2008): 70.

Their minority status in part fuels the work of these anglophone writers in Quebec, where the distinctive linguistic constellation further enhances their language sensibilities. Montreal writers in particular draw inspiration from the English-French duality, as does Gail Scott, who describes herself as "an anglophone writer who wishes to write with the sound of French in her ear, the better to narratively frame her own language/culture from a certain critical distance."[114] With "My Montreal: Notes of an Anglo-Québécois Writer" she has produced a kind of manifesto for the contemporary Anglo writer, in which she explains why

> [...] an anglo writer of my generation, must, in order to express the Québec of this last quarter-century – the Québec of referenda, of economic downsizing – participate in and ultimately address, two often clashing, but also mutually nourishing cultures, simultaneously.[115]

The new Anglo-Québécois literature – 'new' because, while English language writing has existed for a long time in Quebec, claiming its Québécois membership is only a relatively young phenomenon – is thus one marked by contact and exchange.

Things are changing. With the redefinition of Quebec as a francophone society, anglophone writers also need to re-evaluate their relationship with the dominant cultural group, and since the 1980s they are said to be generally "open to francophone aspirations and interested in participating in Quebec society."[116] In the works of Anglo-Québécois authors a certain *"reterritorialisation de l'anglais en sol québécois"*[117] manifests itself according to Catherine Leclerc and Sherry Simon, whose article *"Zones de contact: nouveaux regards sur la littérature anglo-québécoise"* in a 2005 issue of the scholarly journal *Voix et images* is itself a sign of recognition for this new kind of English-language writing in Quebec. Other forms of acknowledgement for Anglo-Québécois literature by francophone literary institutions include the fact that in 2004 the *Grand prix du livre de Montréal* was given for the first time to an anglophone writer – David Solway (*Franklin's Passage*). The post-referendum years have featured some further 'firsts' in Quebec history, like the well-attended *Write Pour Ecrire*, in which francophone and anglophone writers read works of artists from the other language group to enthusiastic audiences of both languages.[118]

---

[114] SCOTT, 5.
[115] SCOTT, 7.
[116] Linda Leith cited in Catherine LECLERC and Sherry SIMON. "Zones de contact: nouveaux regards sur la littérature anglo-québécoise." *Voix et images* 30.3 (2005): 17.
[117] LECLERC and SIMON, 20.
[118] Cf. SCOTT, 9.

In 2004, a small anthology entitled *Montréal, la marge au cœur* brought together short stories (all in French, one in translation) in which four francophone and one anglophone writer tell their personal vision of the city. What these authors do not have in common is the mother tongue, but they are connected through their shared experience of Montreal. It is thus their affiliation to the city that serves Anglophones and Francophones as a 'contact zone.'[119] The next chapter follows Proulx's and Bissoondath's characters and examines their experiences in this contact zone.

---

[119] Cf. LECLERC and SIMON, 28.

4. Contact Zones / *Zones de contact*

> [V]ivre avec l'autre, avec l'étranger, nous confronte à la possibilité ou non *d'être un autre*. Il ne s'agit pas simplement – humanistement – de notre aptitude à accepter l'autre ; mais *d'être à sa place*, ce qui revient à se penser et à se faire autre à soi-même […]. A partir de l'autre, je me réconcilie avec ma propre altérité-étrangeté.
> - Julia Kristeva[120] -

> [N]o identity can ever exist by itself and without an array of opposites, negatives, oppositions.
> - Edward Said[121] -

Psychoanalyst Julia Kristeva, in the spirit of Rimbaud's famous formula "*Je est un autre*," argues that alterity is an inextricable component of self-construction and suggests that one has to acknowledge the otherness external to oneself in order to engage the otherness within oneself and vice versa. Similarly, Edward Said emphasises that identification is a relational process that requires, by definition, more than one identity in order to exist. In the Canadian imagination the Other occupies a peculiar place, as it is at times perceived as a menace and at others as an inherent feature of the national collective consciousness; the latter is particularly true if one considers that Canada frequently casts itself as the 'Other,' especially in contrast to the US. The authors of *Canadian Studies in the New Millennium* (2008) describe the Other as an "enduring theme in the study of Canada," on which they elaborate in the following:

> Dimensions of this theme relate to both internal and external levels of interaction. Examples of the Other include survival in Canada's forebidding [*sic*] geography, proximity to the sometimes overwhelming United States, the persistence of ethno-linguistic divisions (such as francophone language and culture), the status of Aboriginal peoples, and cultural survival in the face of fragmentation.[122]

However, *l'Autre* has had to arduously claim its presence, notably in the Quebec collectivity, where the dominant discourse about Québécois culture prior to the 1980s did not easily include other cultures, not even "*l'Autre par excellence*

---

[120] Julia KRISTEVA. *Etrangers à nous-mêmes*. Paris: Gallimard, 1988. 25, 269.
[121] Edward SAID. *Culture and Imperialism*. NY: Knopf, 1993. 52.
[122] Patrick JAMES and Mark KASOFF. "Future Prospects." In *Canadian Studies in the New Millennium*. Eds. Patrick James and Mark Kasoff. Toronto: U of Toronto P, 2008. 277-78.

(=l'Anglais)."[123] One can discern a shift in paradigms since the 1980s, when writers turned away from the nationalist themes so prevalent in the 1960s and 1970s, and began to investigate what a *pure laine* mindset had previously defined as 'other.' Today, writers and critics aware of Montreal's pluriethnic reality respond to the increasing prominence of (im)migrant literature and the fact that a multiplicity of Others has replaced the former English-French binarism.[124]

The dynamic interrelation of alterities is emblematic of Montreal. The city provides a space where Self and Other meet, an inevitable contact zone; originally, the term 'contact zone' was introduced by Mary Louise Pratt to

> [...] refer to social spaces where cultures meet, clash, and grapple with each other, often in contexts of highly asymmetrical relations of power, such as colonialism, slavery, or their aftermaths as they are lived out in many parts of the world today.[125]

Such a space of contact and confrontation is the Montreal of *Les Aurores montréales*, in which Proulx takes stock of the diversity and urban hybridity of the city. Connecting the individual stories, the metropolis itself is the true hero of the collection and serves as "a backdrop for a postmodern human mosaic at the end of the twentieth century."[126] Not only does the book offer a mosaic of Montreal society, the stories are also colourful in the literal sense of the word. There are six short stories that contain colour(s) in their title and which, moreover, are typographically set off from the rest of the narratives through their being written in italics. In addition, three of these stories, brimming over with intertextual references, are dedicated to neo-Québécois authors, namely to Ying Chen (*"Jaune et blanc"*), Marco Micone (*"Rose et blanc"*) and Dany Laferrière (*"Noir et blanc"*). Critics have named the six 'colour stories' respectively *"nouvelles chromatiques"* (chromatic stories) or "prologues" that group together stories into a certain thematic section.[127]

The very first story, *"Gris et blanc,"* announces the tone for the entire collection and establishes a setting that is defined by its nordicity, modernity and prosperity: "*Ça s'appelle Montréal. C'est un endroit nordique et extrêmement civilisé. Toutes les autos s'arrêtent à tous les feux rouges et les rires sont interdits passé cer-*

---

[123] Peter KLAUS. "Introduction." *Neue Romania* 18 (1997): 6.
[124] On this see also chapter 4.1.
[125] Mary Louise PRATT. "Arts of the Contact Zone." In *Academic Discourse: Readings for Argument and Analysis*. Ed. Gail Stygall. 3rd ed. Mason, Ohio: Thomson Custom Publishing, 2002. 615.
[126] EIBL. "The French-Canadian Short Prose Narrative." (2008), 454.
[127] Cf. Myriam AMRANE. "*Les aurores montréales* de Monique Proulx ou l'appropriation d'un lieu de vie." *Synergies Algérie* 4 (2009): 151. See also SHIRINIAN, 2.

taines heures."[128] The first-person narrator is an adolescent boy who has recently emigrated from Costa Rica and who has now become a third partner in the relationship of Montreal's two solitudes. As soon as he is settled, he cannot help but be immersed in the city's linguistic duality: "*Je sais déjà plein de mots anglais, comme fast, fast.*"[129] Given that time is proverbially money, it is a sign of the historical status of the English language as the language of (material) success in Montreal – which it continues to be to a considerable extent – that such words constitute the first items of the narrator's English vocabulary.

Having been placed in a North American consumer society, the young Hispanophone gauges his new life by possessions,[130] telling his friend Manu, to whom he is writing, about their sofa, new mattress, two tables, four chairs and a marvellous refrigerator that could hold a great number of tortillas. The refrigerator symbolises the immigrant's ambiguous place between hardship and hope, nostalgia and disenchantment. On the one hand, the snoring of the refrigerator repeatedly wakes him up, but on the other, the noise reminds him of the sea, at least in his dreams. While it connects his past to the present, the 'there' of poverty and the promising 'here,' the fridge – a fridge that can contain things like enormous chunks of beef of a tenderness one would not find, the boy maintains, in Puerto Quepos – makes the narrator remember that they have chosen their exile and that they traded the sea for the vast and grey cityscape of Montreal. Yet, a full refrigerator indicates economic well-being and for this one is willing to put up with its "*grondement terrible*," because, after all, "*le chemin vers la richesse est rempli de bruits qui n'effraient pas l'oreille du brave.*"[131]

Again and again the boy talks about wealth and the road to riches, which is a cold one in Montreal and which he can only bear by wearing "three Montreal wool sweaters," though it is only November. The "*trois chandails en laine de Montréal*,"[132] or indeed any reference to *laine* in Quebec, conjure up almost automatically the expression *pure laine*, as in *Québécois pure laine*, which denotes a francophone Quebecer of French-Canadian ancestry. Proulx thus plays with the notion of the superposi-

---

[128] Monique PROULX. *Les Aurores montréales*. 2ᵉ éd. Montréal: Boréal compact, 1997. 7 (forthwith abbreviated as *AM*).
[129] PROULX, *AM*, 8.
[130] This is a recurrent trope in migrant writing. See Rosemary M. GEORGE. *The Politics of Home: Postcolonial Relocations and Twenty-First Century Fiction*. Cambridge: Cambridge UP, 1996 (e.g. page 2 and 133).
[131] PROULX, *AM*, 7, 8.
[132] PROULX, *AM*, 7.

tion of three cultures and languages that the narrator experiences as an immigrant in Montreal.

Humour, in particular in the form of irony, which is frequently employed in the collection as a means of deconstructing anxiety and cultural alienation, runs virtually like a red thread through all of the narratives. In *"Gris et blanc"* irony is expressed through the naïveté of the first-person narrator, who mistakes the Saint Lawrence river for the sea, for instance, but a sea that, according to him, is grey and so modern that it does not smell of living things. Apart from the coldness of the place, it is the grey that upsets him most, and being surrounded by grey houses, grey asphalt and a grey school leads him to the conclusion that grey is the national colour. While this declaration may reflect the monochrome life of many immigrants, Proulx exploits the resources of colour symbolism and ends on a positive note with *la beauté blanche*, that is snow, which makes everything white that was previously grey. Snow is found in several of the short stories as a symbol of hope that carries the possibility for transformation. In the boy's eyes snow obscures Montreal's physical and metaphorical greyness in *"Gris et blanc,"* whereas in the story *"Blanc"* it snows when the narrator looks hopefully into the future after the sorrow the death of her recent anglophone friend has caused her.

As far as structure is concerned, the opening narrative is also a typical story à la Proulx with a little surprise twist at the end. Subsequent to the euphoria engendered by his first experience of snow, the narrator addresses his friend by concluding, *"Ah, dure assez longtemps, Manu, fais durer ta vie de chien jusqu'à ce que je puisse te faire venir ici, avec moi, pour jouer dans la neige."*[133] While the feeling that they were leading a dog's life, a life of misery, probably prompted the family to emigrate to Quebec in pursuit of a brighter future, a closer examination of the story makes clear the double entendre of *"ta vie de chien,"* because the 'I' of the story is, in fact, writing to his dog Manu.

The title of *"Gris et blanc,"* the first of the six 'colour stories,' is ambiguous as well. Since the narrator invites his dog to come and play in the snow, which synecdochically stands for the city, *blanc* obviously refers to Montreal – despite the boy's impression that everything is grey there. Grey, in turn, may either designate memories of a former "dog's life" or the greyness of the reality as lived by migrants in

---

[133] PROULX, *AM*, 9.

Montreal, before "*l'odeur de la richesse commence [...] à s'infiltrer*"[134] and before they themselves have managed to filter, so to speak, into Quebec society. Either way, both colours can ultimately be attributed to Montreal.

The other five 'colour stories' of *Les Aurores montréales* further contribute to the portrayal of a multi-hued Montreal. By using *blanc* in each title of the six short narratives in question, Proulx probably wants to convey more than just the whiteness as occasioned by the snow that is so characteristic of the city. Although whiteness, like snow, is positively connoted, it might equally allude to white hegemony, implying that however colourful Montreal's mosaic of diverse peoples may be, its basic tint is still predominantly white. Five of the six stories represent immigrants and how they interact in and with the metropolis, bringing their own colours (*gris, jaune, rose, noir* and *rouge*) to Montreal (*blanc*) that absorbs them all in the end. Immigrants do not figure in *Blanc*, the book's last story, where categories such as 'Montrealer' or 'foreigner' are finally obliterated.[135] Similar to the colour white, which reflects the absence of colour at the same time as it is a combination of all colours of the spectrum, Montreal, blending a variety of people and ethnicities, becomes "*un espace vierge*,"[136] a virgin space, where Self and Other merge.

In her short stories Proulx wilfully provokes the confrontation of the self with the other. Although it is sometimes a painful encounter, it may still result in an eventual revelation situated somewhere between resentfulness, resignation and wisdom. For Pratt, this is the normal experience in the contact zone: "Along with rage, incomprehension, and pain, there [are] exhilarating moments of wonder and revelation, mutual understanding, and new wisdom – the joys of the contact zone."[137] Like Proulx, Bissoondath explores this zone in his self-appointed mission: "the demystification of the Other."[138] A first step towards achieving his goal is to grapple with difference, because, as he puts it,

> [...] so long as there's difference, there's fear. And that will manifest itself in various ways. We're most at ease with the familiar; it's a normal human reaction. How far you take that reaction, how you deal with that unease, is the question. I think it's essential for writers to approach difference – if you don't, what are you going to write about?[139]

---

[134] Ibid.
[135] For a detailed discussion of the short story "*Blanc*" see chapter 4.7.
[136] PROULX, *AM*, 239.
[137] PRATT, 626.
[138] Qtd. in KRUK, 67.
[139] Qtd. in KRUK, 68.

Furthermore, "the recognition of difference is," according to the Canadian philosopher Charles Taylor, "not only a moral but a vital human need in that it is tied up with the process of identity construction."[140]

Identity does not seem to be of much concern to the protagonist of *Doing the Heart Good*, whose self-confidence frequently borders on obdurateness. In Alistair Mackenzie, a staunch believer in his own opinion and principles, Bissoondath chose a particularly interesting character to place in situations in which he is forced to deal with differences of various kinds. Having to face the diversity of his environment, Mackenzie is compelled to readjust his attitudes and convictions as he is confronted, among other things, by a blind student, a dwarfish accountant and people who do not speak his language. A reviewer of the novel characterises Mackenzie as "cranky, self-absorbed, prejudiced, and [...] a near-stereotypical old Anglo fart" who "engages in a one-sided anti-French grudge match with his inoffensive Québécois upstairs tenant."[141] While this unflattering judgment hits the nail on its head in several respects, the opening pages of the novel provide a more accurate introduction to the protagonist and the key themes of *Doing the Heart Good*.

"A breathless silence."[142] These are both the first and next to last words of the novel that occur after Mackenzie has just gone through some major or minor turning point in his life and is left, for a moment, in a state of perplexity. It is a sort of calm after the storm that overcomes him, which is his normal reaction to change, to which he is completely averse, in line with his usual lack of open-mindedness. In the beginning the rather uneasy calm results from his house having been reduced to ashes and his subsequent move to his daughter's home, even though he says, "I did all I could to avoid ending up here."[143] This is how the novel starts, told by Mackenzie in first-person narration as he looks back at his life by writing down some episodes of it.

Moreover, it is Christmas Eve and Alistair Mackenzie 'celebrates'

> the six-month anniversary of the night that brought me here, six months during which Agnes, her husband and her son have grown accustomed to addressing me in a low shout. This speaking to me as if I were at the far end of a large room no longer requires great effort of them, it now comes quite naturally. Even so, and despite the latest technological

---

[140] Qtd. in Martin GENETSCH. *The Texture of Identity: The Fiction of MG Vassanji, Neil Bissoondath and Rohinton Mistry*. Toronto: Tsar Publications, 2007. 3.

[141] Joan BARFOOT. "*Doing the Heart Good* by Neil Bissoondath." *Quill & Quire* March 2002. St. Joseph Media Inc. 4 Sept. 2009 <http://www.quillandquire.com/reviews/review.cfm?review_id=2631>.

[142] BISSOONDATH, *DHG*, 1, 143, 345. See moreover page 47, where the narrator also uses the adjective "breathless" to qualify the silence and remarks, "There is something suspicious about it."

[143] BISSOONDATH, *DHG*, 1.

contraption plugged into my ear, words reach me like a whisper through a straw. Mine is the only voice that resounds with any clarity in my head, the only voice I truly hear.[144]

This introductory paragraph to his narrative sheds light on several of the protagonist's characteristics, especially with regard to how he interacts with people around him. To begin with, the fact that he mentions his son-in-law Jacques and his grandson François in relation to his daughter Agnes (*her* husband, *her* son) instead of to himself, shows that there is still distance between them, because at this stage he has not had the benefits of hindsight that he reaches in the end through the reflection on his life. Secondly, the passage hints at another of his 'qualities,' namely his unwillingness to reconsider his rigid views, which indeed requires his family to address him in low shouts, as talking to him is often comparable to talking to a brick wall. Not surprisingly then, his own voice is the only one he truly hears and mostly one gets the impression that he does not even want to listen to any others that might call into question his preconceived notions. In fact, Mackenzie more than once seriously considers turning off his hearing aid to avoid or escape from an unpleasant conversation, "but that would be an ugly thing to do,"[145] his conscience objects.

"A breathless silence" thus also refers to one of the novel's most central themes and preoccupations: communication, or rather the lack of it. Throughout the novel there are numerous instances that demonstrate that conversation is an art in which Mackenzie is "neither gifted nor versed" and that with him, "small talk tends to grow smaller."[146] It is an indication of his self-importance that the verbal exchange of ideas is first and foremost a chore for him. As a literature professor, the narrator is clearly more in the habit of lecturing than being lectured to. Luckily, there is his wife Mary, a counterforce to his self-complacency, to keep alive his sense of foolishness and Mackenzie good-humouredly includes her criticism in his narrative, as in:

> Mary often said it was a wonder I never dislocated my shoulder trying to pat myself on the back. One morning, wishing to loosen up my stiff, underexercised muscles, I performed a few toe-touches before the bedroom mirror. Mary came in, took one look at me, and accused me of bowing myself in adoration. I'm not a bad fellow, she always said, simply one whose attention and sympathy are most easily stirred by his own achievements.[147]

In addition to his deficiency in taking an interest in other people's views, non-dialogue may equally be his way to shun confrontation; at one point he admits, "The

---

[144] Ibid.
[145] BISSOONDATH, *DHG*, 181. Sometimes his conscience remains silent, however, and he does turn it off (cf. 2).
[146] BISSOONDATH, *DHG*, 60, 175.
[147] BISSOONDATH, *DHG*, 19.

silence I'm accustomed to is a cocoon, its membrane constantly pressed by disturbance near and far."[148]

Above all, dysfunctional communication manifests itself in Mackenzie's categorical refusal to speak (and understand) French. Without doubt he does have some knowledge of French, as evidenced by the following short dialogue with his grandson, for example:

- 'Grand-papa, m'as-tu acheté un cadeau?'
- 'A *cadeau*? Have I bought you a gift? Well now, let's see. A gift for François. Oh dear me, how could I have forgotten?'[149]

But it seems to be a matter of principle for him to stick to his own language, regardless of how little effort it would have required to reply in French, in everyday situations such as when a security guard addresses him in a shopping mall:

- 'Monsieur? Ça va?'
- 'I'm fine, thank you.'[150]

Motivations that propel the protagonist to feign complete ignorance of the majority language in Quebec will be analysed in more detail in chapter 4.6.

Apart from his interactions with Jacques and François, Mackenzie's relationship to his former francophone upstairs neighbour Tremblay highlights best his linguistic idiosyncrasies. As early as on page two, Tremblay is introduced to the story and continues to appear throughout the narrative as the protagonist's primary target of the latter's anti-French stance. Their (unilateral) disputes – one should add that Tremblay is loquacious, peaceable and ultimately saves Mackenzie's life – form the crux of the francophone-anglophone dichotomy the novel is chiefly concerned with.

At one point Mackenzie describes his relationship with Tremblay in the following terms: "We have been uneasy neighbours for longer than I care to remember. We have watched each other growing infirm."[151] Underlying this statement is the novel's implied message that the former English-French antagonism has likewise grown infirm in Quebec. The paradigm shift is exemplified by Mackenzie's gradual change in his dealings with Tremblay, Jacques and the new generation of (bilingual) Francophones as represented by his grandson François. Again, the process involves cross-cultural (and -linguistic) communication that the narrator certainly does not seek voluntarily. He terminates his first mention of Tremblay by saying:

---

[148] BISSOONDATH, *DHG*, 47.
[149] BISSOONDATH, *DHG*, 9.
[150] BISSOONDATH, *DHG*, 11.
[151] BISSOONDATH, *DHG*, 299.

> We always had such a difficult time with each other face to face. Even with the help of new telephone technology for the deaf, I fear I would catch only every second or third word of his.
>
> I am happier burying my nose in my sleeve, filling my mind with the scent of the countless people who've entered my life, stayed a while, then left.[152]

By now it should be clear that his catching "only every second or third word" refers as much to a metaphorical deafness as to a physical one.

That Mackenzie prefers burying his nose in his sleeve illustrates a number of things. First of all, the sleeve belongs to faded cotton pyjamas which are among the few things besides his war medals that were saved from the ravaging of the flames. He clings to them with a tenacity that shows that he does not easily let go of the past and a sheltered existence devoid of any uncomfortable opposition. Clothes often function as a symbol and expression of identity; in this case they are used to demonstrate Mackenzie's reluctance to change and to adopt new views after he has been so agreeably settled with his old ones. Complaining about being "encased in the unfamiliarity of new garments," which is no small thing for a man his age, he argues that "[i]t's like assuming a new skin after decades of breaking in the old."[153] Furthermore, the pyjamas' smoky scent evokes memories of the past, which indicates the importance of memory as another of the book's key preoccupations. His memories naturally include the encounters with the characters that people the novel. How the narrator interacts with those "who've entered [his] life, stayed a while, then left" and what impact they, in turn, have had on his life can be understood better by applying cultural concepts such as multi-, inter- and transculturalism.

4.1. Multiculturalism, Interculturalism and Transculturalism

Alistair Mackenzie has a hard time accepting difference; he may tolerate it, but that is definitely not the same, as Bissoondath emphasises in the call he submits in *Selling Illusions* for an "*accepting* society":

> Acceptance [...] requires true understanding, recognition over time that the obvious difference – the accent, the skin colour, the crossed eyes, the large nose – are mere decorations on the person beneath. It is a meeting of peoples that delves under the surface to a knowledge of the full humanity of the other.

---

[152] BISSOONDATH, *DHG*, 3.
[153] BISSOONDATH, *DHG*, 1-2.

Tolerance, on the other hand, is far more fragile, for it requires not knowledge but wilful ignorance, [...] but tolerance is clearly insufficient in the building of a cohesive society. A far greater goal to strive for would be an *accepting* society.[154]

In general, Bissoondath criticises Canada's official multiculturalism – which was adopted in 1971 under the premiership of Pierre Elliot Trudeau and substituted biculturalism – for doing Canadians a disservice, since it fails to provide any sense of unity.[155] The Canadian concept of multiculturalism is epitomised by the image of the cultural mosaic consisting of a diversity of cultures which may live next to each other in peaceful co-existence, while each group remains relatively closed and without necessarily influencing others. Some critics perceive the term multiculturalism as a mere disguise for a plurality of monocultures. Among these critics is Homi Bhabha, who argues that multiculturalism or cultural diversity is based on the "separation of totalized cultures that live unsullied by the intertextuality of their historical locations, safe in the Utopianism of a mythic memory of a unique collective identity."[156] Bhabha thus rejects 'cultural diversity,' because, in his understanding of the phrase, it treats cultures as pre-given entities. Instead of an essentialist approach to culture he advocates a focus on 'cultural difference,' which suggests the internal complexity of cultures and their openness and unfixity.[157]

Quebec objected to Canada's multicultural policy for different reasons. For Quebec, Trudeau's policy meant a further consolidation of anglophone hegemony and an undermining of the province's special status, especially as far as the French language was concerned. Some argued that Trudeau's vision boiled down to an "insidious and steady shift away from biculturalism towards a crushing of Francophones' special needs under the political weight of multiculturalism,"[158] devised as an attempt to gain so-called ethnic votes. By contrast, Quebec defines itself as a

---

[154] Neil BISSOONDATH. *Selling Illusions: The Cult of Multiculturalism in Canada*. Toronto: Penguin Books, 1994. 191-92.

[155] Faye Hammill submits a similar critique and talks about multiculturalism's divisiveness and its encouraging ghettoisation and stereotyping. "Yet," she writes, "despite these various critiques of multiculturalism, its core values of respect and tolerance are, on the whole, widely accepted in Canada." (Faye HAMMILL. *Canadian Literature*. Edinburgh: Edinburgh UP, 2007. 28).

[156] Homi K. BHABHA. "Cultural Diversity and Cultural Differences." In *The Post-Colonial Studies Reader*. Eds. Bill Ashcroft, Gareth Griffiths and Helen Tiffin. London: Routledge, 1995. 206.

[157] Cf. Jonathan RUTHERFORD. Ed. "The Third Space: Interview with Homi Bhabha." In *Identity: Community, Culture, Difference*. London: Lawrence & Wishart, 1990. 207-9.

[158] Qtd. in Helmut J. VOLLMER. "Französierung und Herkunftssprachen in Québec – Modelle und Perspektiven einer pluriethnischen Gesellschaft." *Grenzgänge* 3 (1995): 65.

pluriethnic society[159] and promotes the concept of interculturalism, which does not stress the individuality of cultural groups but the reciprocity and exchange between them. Interculturalism assumes the inherent openness of a culture that automatically engenders a dialogue once a culture is exposed to another. Also, it differs fundamentally from the ideology of multiculturalism in that it does not place all cultures on the same level, but organises them on the basis of a common civic culture, which, in Quebec's case, is a majority French-speaking one, into which everybody is required to integrate. Moreover, the idea of interculturalism responds more to the actual reality of the dynamic nature of culture and the resulting interrelation between different groups living on the same territory.

Another concept that takes into account the essential heterogeneity of cultures, their interconnectedness and their being always in process is captured by the word transculturalism. Wolfgang Welsch introduced[160] the term 'transculturality' to

> describe a strikingly new, contemporary feature of cultures originating from their increased blending. The main idea was that deep differences between cultures are today diminishing more and more, that contemporary cultures are characterized by cross-cutting elements – and in this sense are to be comprehended as transcultural rather than monocultural. It seemed to me (and still does) that the inherited concept of cultures as homogeneous and closed entities has become highly inappropriate in comprehending the constitution of today's cultures.[161]

According to Welsch, then, former conceptions of culture did not sufficiently consider cultures' hybridity and the fact that contact between them leaves both sides modified. This dynamic is also attested by Jean Lamore, who gives the following definition of transculturation:

> [L]a transculturation est un ensemble de transmutations constantes ; elle est créatrice et jamais achevée ; elle est irréversible. Elle est toujours un processus dans lequel on donne quelque chose en échange de ce que l'on reçoit : les deux parties de l'équation s'en trouvent

---

[159] In many respects there are parallels or at least similarities to the basic values of multiculturalism. For a more detailed discussion, see VOLLMER, 69-72. See also OAKES and WARREN, 28.

[160] The term was, however, coined much earlier by the Cuban anthropologist Fernando Ortiz: "Entendemos que el vocablo *transculturación* expresa mejor las diferentes fases del proceso transitivo de una cultura a otra" (Fernando ORTIZ. *Contrapunteo cubano del tabaco y del azúcar*. 1940. Caracas: Biblioteca Ayacucho, 1987. 96). Moreover, Welsch uses the term 'transculturality' about ten years after Quebec authors such as Berrouet-Oriol or Lamore. Chronologically, the term thus originated in Cuba, before reaching Quebec and later Germany.

[161] Wolfgang WELSCH. "On the Acquisition and Possession of Commonalities." In *Transcultural English Studies: Theories, Fictions, Realities*. Eds. Frank Schulze-Engler and Sissy Helff. Amsterdam: Rodopi, 2009. 4. See also: Wolfgang WELSCH. "Transkulturalität: Zur veränderten Verfassung heutiger Kulturen." In *Hybridkultur: Medien, Netze, Künste*. Eds. Irmela Schneider and Christian W. Thomsen. Köln: Wienand, 1997. 71.

modifiées. Il en émerge une réalité nouvelle, qui n'est pas une mosaïque de caractères, mais un phénomène nouveau, original et indépendant.[162]

The phenomenon that Lamore describes is similar to Bhabha's 'third space' – a new reality that is not just the composition of its elements, and thus quite unlike a mosaic. To illustrate a non-hierarchical model of culture which allows for multiplicities and their ramifications, Deleuze and Guattari borrowed the image of the rhizome from botany.[163] Their rhizome denotes a network where there is no centre but centres, and which annihilates any false universality or illusory purity. In conclusion, one could say that these theories about transculture, cross-culturality and hybridity all encourage the argument that the francophone monoculture of urban Quebec is "contaminated," even to the point of unsettling such categories as Self and Other.

4.2. Self and Other – Initiation to the Kingdom of Babel

> Even in our solitudes, our autonomous diversities, we have spoken of our attachment to the ideas of justice and peace and self-determination. We are involved with each other in a dialectic of community and society in which no single identity defines us. […] There is no single ghetto into which we can withdraw and still be whole.[164]

The protagonist in the title piece of Proulx's *Les Aurores montréales* is entangled in an identity crisis, which gets further enhanced by the transcultural processes that are going on everywhere around him in the city. Laurel, a sixteen year old boy whose parents are separated, has recently moved from his father's to his mother's home and is not sure where he belongs. In order to compensate this lack, he develops a monomaniacal obsession, his "Cause," as he puts it, that is: *"Défendre le Montréal français contre les Envahisseurs."*[165] Haunted by the fantasy of a pure francophone Montreal,

---

[162] Jean LAMORE. "Transculturation: naissance d'un mot." *Vice Versa* 21 (1987): 18.
[163] See Deleuze and Guattari cited in Domenic BENEVENTI. "Lost in the City: The Montreal Novels of Régine Robin and Robert Majzels." In *Downtown Canada: Writing Canadian Cities*. Eds. Justin D. Edwards and Douglas Ivison. Toronto: U of Toronto P, 2005. 113.
[164] Myrna KOSTASH. "Imagination, Representation, and Culture." In *Literary Pluralities*. Ed. Christl Verduyn. Peterborough: Broadview Press, 1998. 94.
[165] PROULX, *AM*, 160.

Laurel's mission to defend his home town against "the Invaders" results in his plan to write *"un vrai livre sur le vrai visage désolant du nouveau Montréal."*[166]

If it were possible, Laurel would certainly prefer to withdraw into a homogeneous French-speaking ghetto to be spared any contact with the Invaders that threaten the world of someone who reads *"des livres québécois-de-langue-française à l'exclusion de tous les autres."*[167] Yet, Montreal is so permeated by foreignness and alterity that all he can do is to write down vengeful phrases in his notebook as he moves about the city like a *"fébrile guérillero traquant les indices incriminants."*[168] In the Avenue du Parc, for instance, which the protagonist describes as a linguistic battlefield and ugly micro-Babel, he finds abundant evidence of the presence of his biggest enemy – English. Once, when chancing upon a boy his age who is also frantically taking notes, Laurel overcomes his habitual reserve, and almost extends his hand while feeling his heart soften by the beginning of an authentic friendship. So happy is he to have found a battle companion on the same side of the barricade. Disillusionment is quick to follow as his potential battle companion takes off his headphones, stops copying down the lyrics of a song *"très hard metal et terriblement* English" and asks suspiciously, "What dayawant?" Laurel utters a disconcerted "Exquiouse me," before he retreats, feeling confirmed in his solitude.[169]

Laurel is a staunch Francophone, who could also be counted among Montreal's angryphone faction. His anger probably stems from his insecurity, which is an integral part of the liminal space he occupies both as a son whose loyalties are divided between dissimilar parents and as a teenager crossing the threshold from childhood to adulthood. Not only do the problems of growing up and a natural fear of the unknown destabilise his sense of self; his quest for completeness and unity in the process of identification also prevent him from acknowledging that selfhood is fragmented, fluid and intrinsically heterogeneous.

In vain does he seek uniformity in contemporary Montreal and in his own environment. While he professes to loath difference, Laurel himself is the offspring of two people who could hardly be more antithetical:

---

[166] PROULX, *AM*, 157.
[167] PROULX, *AM*, 160. Moreover, it says that Laurel *"connaît par cœur Michel Tremblay, il a emprunté à Francine Noël son image montréalaise de Babel, il vénère Sylvain Trudel et Gaétan Soucy et Esther Rochon et Louis Hamelin"* (these are all Québécois authors who were born in Quebec).
[168] PROULX, *AM*, 159.
[169] Ibid.

> Son père est un francophone de souche, l'un de ces opiniâtres termites que les marées anglophone et allophone n'ont pas réussi à évincer de la galerie primordiale. [...] Sa mère pourrait être n'importe quoi, à voir la façon dont elle pactise avec l'étrange, dont elle plonge ses racines malléables dans toutes sortes de terreaux suspects. Sa mère habite le quartier grec limitrophe du quartier hassidim, tient un magasin d'aliments naturels chez les Anglais, fait ses emplettes chez les Italiens et couche avec un Chilien.[170]

In his book, he adds, his mother will be called "*Iouniverselle*" and she will disappear early either as a victim of assassination or assimilation, both equally severe crimes in his opinion. His mother's "malleable roots" expand in a culture that basically corresponds to the image of the rhizome, whereas Laurel envisages a single French root[171] that would not, like his father, be swept away by "the anglophone and allophone tides." The main problem with his mother, Laurel elaborates, is that she does not perceive the dangers, the real dangers that are everywhere and that, as he points out, sometimes have nothing to do with language. For him, religious symbols, for example, constitute one such menace. Aware that most individuals construct their sense of identity through some sort of group membership, such as that of a particular linguistic or religious community, Laurel feels threatened by any all too obvious signs of belonging. After all, he himself lacks reference points, which causes him to value all the more his French Canadian heritage.

In diametrical opposition to her son, Iouniverselle "would sell her soul to communicate," which in Laurel's eyes makes her a poor blind lambkin running to its own extermination, although it is he who is blind. Conversely, his mother is not really worried about her son's cultural myopia and regards it as just a phase: "*Tu es un intelligent petit con, mais tu changeras.*"[172] Iouniverselle embraces difference and alterity, which appear in the story to be as *montréalais* as Mount Royal, whereas Laurel is most intimidated by otherness and change. Yet, the revelatory book about the new Montreal that he is planning to write is to be entitled *Les Aurores montréales* and, inspired by the colourful *aurores boréales* or northern polar lights, to convey the constant flux and mixture of diverse colours characterising the city. "*Montréal est une ville qui n'arrête pas de changer, [...] une ville qui additionne tellement les nouveaux visages que l'on perd toujours celui que l'on croyait enfin connaître,*"[173] he writes,

---

[170] PROULX, *AM*, 158.
[171] Edouard Glissant comments, "*La racine unique est celle qui tue autour d'elle alors que le rhizome est la racine qui s'étend à la rencontre d'autres racine*" (Edouard GLISSANT. *Introduction à une poétique du divers*. Paris: Gallimard, 1996. 59).
[172] PROULX, *AM*, 160.
[173] PROULX, *AM*, 164.

implying that the new faces might erase the original face of Montreal that he would so much like to conserve.

That Laurel does not accept the Other goes hand in hand with his inability to admit his personal otherness, one could argue and apply Kristeva who pointed out that it is through *l'Autre* that one becomes reconciled to one's own alterity and strangeness.[174] Stuart Hall likewise asserts that the Other is an inalienable part of any identity formation:

> Above all, and directly contrary to the form in which they are constantly invoked, identities are constructed through, not outside, difference. This entails the radically disturbing recognition that it is only through the relation to the Other, the relation to what it is not, to precisely what it lacks, to what has been called its *constitutive outside* that the 'positive' meaning of any term – and thus its 'identity' – can be constructed.[175]

Before Laurel finally confronts his "constitutive outside," his kind of *alter ego* personified by a neighbourhood boy of Greek origin the protagonist condescendingly names "*Soufflaki*," there is one other place where he accommodates Self and Other: Mount Royal, a neutral space towering above the disorder of the "*royaume de Babel*."[176] Sherry Simon remarks on the special cultural role of Mount Royal:

> It is a place of gathering – not least of languages. As a valued space and as an arena of citizenship, Mount Royal is a unique symbol of the urban ideal, a terrain at once within and outside city territory, participating in the struggle of languages and yet remaining outside of it.[177]

It is there that Laurel is liberated from his rage and that an amazing thing happens to him: "*c'est de sentir peu à peu un étranger s'installer dans son esprit, et d'aimer cet étranger*;" and he concludes that from the perspective of Mount Royal, the metropolis exudes the graceful modernity of a postcard. "*D'ici, Montréal ne fait pas mal.*"[178]

Mount Royal and sushi are Laurel's "*deux oasis qui rendent cette inhospitalière Babel à peu près supportable.*"[179] This is one of several contradictions about the protagonist, who after all seems as much attracted by the unknown as he appears repulsed by it; or perhaps the Japanese who have brought with them such delicious things as sushi do not count among the "Invaders"? Laurel's considerably restricted vision of multiculturalism is equivalent to what Stanley Fish calls 'boutique multicul-

---

[174] See Kristeva quoted at the beginning of chapter 4.
[175] Stuart HALL. "Introduction: Who Needs 'Identity'?" In *Questions of Cultural Identity*. Eds. Stuart Hall and Paul du Gay. London: Sage, 1996. 4-5.
[176] PROULX, *AM*, 157.
[177] SIMON (2006), 191.
[178] PROULX, *AM*, 163.
[179] PROULX, *AM*, 166.

turalism:' "Boutique multiculturalism is the multiculturalism of ethnic restaurants, weekend festivals, and high profile flirtations with the other."[180] Fish could have had Laurel in mind, when he defined a 'boutique multiculturalist' as someone who

> may find something of value in rap music and patronize (pun intended) soul-food restaurants, but he [...] does not take difference seriously because its marks (quaint clothing, atonal music, curious table manners) are for him matters of lifestyle, and as such they should not be allowed to overwhelm the substratum of rationality that makes us all brothers under the skin.[181]

Not only does Laurel *not* take difference seriously, but he feels immensely irritated by ostensible signs of otherness and accordingly dismisses anything that is foreign or that he does not understand. An incident at the Syrian *pâtissier* illustrates this: allured by rosewater and pistachio cream baklavas, another of the delights Montreal holds for him, Laurel frequents a pastry shop run by a Syrian who, every time he is about to mention money, bows low, his hands shaped like a tent in front of his forehead, "*adressant à quelque Moloch ou Tanit barbare une prière muette en forme de piastre.*"[182] Not even the man's impeccable French can help prevent Laurel from finding his behaviour exceedingly disturbing until he discovers that the man's gesture does not betoken some weird fanaticism but that he performs it merely to shade his eyes so that he can read the figures on a shield. The discovery leaves the boy angry at himself, because his stereotypes have not been confirmed.

In order to avoid having to deal with other individuals and their complex identities, Laurel is careful to keep them (and by inference any Other) always at a distance.[183] Until the turning point of the story, brought about by his encounter with Soufflaki, the protagonist does not recognise others in their identity but deindividuates them by employing the impersonal marker of the plural, as in "*Sont gras. Sont cons. Le soir, ils investissent le milieu de la rue [...]. Sont irritants.*"[184] Who are 'they'? The 'Invaders' do not strike one as being real persons but imaginary ones that

---

[180] Stanley FISH. "Boutique Multiculturalism, or Why Liberals Are Incapable of Thinking About Hate Speech." *Critical Inquiry* 23.2 (1997): 378.
[181] FISH, 380, 384.
[182] PROULX, *AM*, 161.
[183] Eibl argues that such behaviour results either in idealised folklorisation or categorical rejection: "Den Anderen auf Distanz zu halten, ihm nicht zu begegnen kann einerseits zu seiner idealisierten Folklorisierung führen, andererseits kann aus dieser Distanzierung aber auch eine breite Dynamik der grundsätzlichen Ablehnung entstehen, vor allem dann, wenn das im menschlichen Selbstverständnis latent vorhandene Begehren nach Einzigartigkeit den Anderen, ob er nun gleich oder anders ist, nicht akzeptieren kann, wenn er nicht die positive Antwort auf das Selbst ist." EIBL (1999), 35.
[184] PROULX, *AM*, 157, 161.

the sixteen-year-old Francophile has appropriated to suit his preconceived ideas. Additionally, 'they' function as a convenient counterpart that he may denigrate to boost his own sense of self.

Also, Laurel apparently likes to imagine himself in the role of the victim, as when he complains about his mother's relationship with the Chilean, Pedro, that "*sa mère lui a toujours préféré les étrangers, toujours.*"[185] Pedro, moreover, gets reduced to his adherence to the Spanish language community: "*Bien entendu qu'il a toujours été mauvais pour elle, cet Hola trop beau qui ne sait pas dire « Hello » même après des années de Québec français.*"[186] It is a typical example of Proulx-esque irony that the anglophobe protagonist criticises his mother's boyfriend for continuing to say '*hola*' instead of 'hello' even after years in French Quebec; perhaps it is another of Laurel's sometimes contradictory features, or might he have forgotten after having grown up in Montreal that 'hello' is not a French word after all?

"Les aurores montréales" is a coming-of-age story or so-called story of initiation, in which the protagonist, usually a child or adolescent, experiences a decisive incident in his or her life that initiates the character into a higher state of awareness in preparation for the adult world. In Laurel's case, the epiphantic moment is triggered by the long-feared confrontation with some boys from his neighbourhood: "*Sont bouclés. Sont gras. Sont cinq. Il a marché, comme un imbécile, directement au centre de leur toile. Laurel serre contre lui son cahier rouge, dérisoire bouclier.*"[187] The hero of the story keeps his notebook – a rather pathetic shield, as he notes – pressed against himself the way he clutches his prejudices to shield himself from the real world and its unpredictability. Similar to his notebook and prejudices, such measures prove futile and the boys advance to address him. At first, Laurel does not understand or does not want to understand them. In his terror he even resorts to the enemy's language to enquire, "What?"

> « Bienvenue à Montréal », dit Soufflaki. Laurel les regarde à tour de rôle : il se sent come au théâtre, comme aux sushis devant les énigmatiques Japonais. Les cinq garçons ont bizarrement le visage barré par un sourire.[188]

This marks the protagonist's initiation to the new Montreal he altogether failed to depict in his ill-conceived book. It is also interesting that although Laurel asks Soufflaki in English to repeat himself, Soufflaki welcomes him in French, which shows that

---

[185] PROULX, *AM*, 166.
[186] PROULX, *AM*, 164.
[187] PROULX, *AM*, 167.
[188] PROULX, *AM*, 168.

Laurel was mistaken in what he believed to be a threat to francophone Montreal. Furthermore, this act of welcoming the main character to his own home town indicates again how blurred the boundaries between Self and Other are. As the new arrival in the district, it is Laurel who is the 'immigrant' or 'Invader,' thus in the end he assumes the identity he formerly projected onto the Other.

Naturally this has to be digested by Laurel. Plausibly, therefore, the short story finishes with the boy dealing with his own ignorance:

> Laurel ne comprend pas ce qu'il ressent, quel est ce trou à l'intérieur de lui, ce gouffre de perplexité et d'ignorance. Il a jeté son cahier rouge dans la poubelle. Il ne sait rien, il faut repartir à zéro. La seule chose qu'il sait, c'est qu'il doit se lever, maintenant, et aller prendre Pauline dans ses bras pour la consoler.[189]

Not only his notebook, but his prejudices finally get discarded. In several short stories Proulx advocates the possibility of starting anew, which seems to be the only other remedy apart from humour against whatever dreary situation one might encounter. The story "*Blanc*" also suggests "*repartir à zéro*" as a method to overcome the historically-conditioned remnants of English-French enmity. In "Les aurores montréales" the boy's readiness to rise and console his mother manifests an awakening understanding of the value of true communication and an acknowledgment of the fact that people are unavoidably linked with each other "in a dialectic of community and society." At an earlier point the narrative even hints at Laurel's willingness to voluntarily serve the exclusively anglophone clientele of Iouniverselle's store. As for the protagonist's identity turmoil, his initiation to Montreal culminates in the awareness that "[b]eing at home in the city means having the privilege of finding oneself disoriented in it, being offered the opportunity to be destabilized."[190]

---

[189] Ibid.
[190] SIMON (2006), 200.

4.3. Montreal's Significant Other(s)

> Je suis duel [...] Je suis de deux nations, de deux imaginaires [...] Je suis culturel, et non pas un demiculturel – interculturel ou transculturel [...] J'écris pour me donner tel que je suis [...] Je t'offre de nouvelles références, une autre vision de la vie d'ici et d'ailleurs. Je suis une autre voix qui vient par une autre voie.
> - Antonio D'Alfonso[191] -

"[E]xoticism is merely the unknown,"[192] Alistair Mackenzie's world-travelling brother-in-law realises towards the end of his life. Montreal may appear exotic from many different angles, since it accommodates such a large variety of Others and their voices. For some, this aspect of the metropolis holds a great charm and they will welcome diversity with open arms, just like the protagonist of the short story "Jouer avec un chat": "*Il sera heureux, ici. [...] Tout à l'heure il a bu des espressos avec un Italien, de la retsina avec un Grec, il a des frères inconnus partout qui ne demandent qu'à pleurer et à rire avec lui. Il marche dans l'amour du genre humain et de Montréal.*"[193] Yet, others are unnerved by the unfamiliar and shocked by "*mille monstruosités citadines (« Mon Dieu! La fille a les cheveux roses... Ma parole, ce type se promène quasiment TOUT NU!... As-tu vu, c'est tous des nègres, les chauffeurs de taxi...»).*"[194]

Anglophones remain Montreal's principal Other (or other Self), as Anglo- and Franco-Montrealers have been bound to each other in a kind of forced marriage for centuries. Still, for a Quebecer coming from somewhere else in the province, *les Anglais* occasionally also continue to be somewhat exotic. In "Le futile et l'essential," a middle-aged woman from rural Quebec visits her daughter in Montreal, bringing with her a list of places and tourist 'musts' that Mrs Chapleau, "Monique's husband's cousin's wife who has a sister who often comes to Montreal," kindly drew up for her. Starting with such sights as the botanical gardens, the Musée des beaux-arts or the Olympic Stadium, the list also includes:

- Les boutiques chic de la rue Laurier, continuait studieusement Fabienne, les smoked meat de chez Saint-Laurent boulevard Schwartz...

---

[191] Qtd. in Louise GAUTHIER. *La mémoire sans frontières: Emile Ollivier, Naïm Kattan et les écrivains migrants au Québec.* Sainte-Foy: Editions de l'IQRC, 1997. 17.
[192] BISSOONDATH, *DHG*, 70.
[193] PROULX, *AM*, 23.
[194] PROULX, *AM*, 40.

- Chez Schwartz boulevard Saint-Laurent, rectifia mollement Martine.
- ... le cimetière Mont-Royal, le quartier des Anglais, le...
Martine éclata de rire, un rire plein de soufre et de désespoir.
- Le quartier des Anglais ?
- Mais... oui ! dit Fabienne. Tu sais bien, dans l'Ouest, Ouestmoont ça s'appelle...[195]

With slightly vexed amusement Martine imagines her mother tracking down *les Anglais*, armed with her camera:

> Oui, il était extrêmement facile de l'imaginer, Fabienne son petit chapeau et son appareil photographique faisant irruption chez des quidams de Trafalgar Heights, à Westmount, martelant le heurtoir en or massif de quelques maisonnettes de trois millions de dollar pour s'enquérir poliment : Êtes-vous un Anglais ?... *May I take a photography ?*...
> - Mais il y en a partout, des Anglais, éclata Martine. Je peux te présenter ceux de l'appartement d'en bas, si tu veux !...[196]

To her daughter's last proposition, to be introduced to the English people of the apartment downstairs, Fabienne does not even react, because that would simply be too mundane.

Montreal is not Quebec. The pluralistic metropolis is distinct from the rest of the province and from Quebec City, the capital and sort of *pars pro toto* for Quebec in that the number of Anglophones resident there has been dwindling, for example. In fact, for those accustomed to the cosmopolitan city the rest of the country possibly gives a rather monolithic impression. In a conversation with Anglo-Canadian writer Margaret Atwood, Victor-Lévy Beaulieu, a well-known figure on the Quebec literary scene, said that he had no direct contact with the English language in his childhood and he described his first experience with an Anglophone as a culture shock:

> The only anglophone I saw in the whole of my childhood was in Trois-Pistoles: every fall, [Planter's] sent Mr. Peanut on tour around the province. [...] We wanted to know if he was the real Mr. Peanut or just someone disguised as a peanut [...] and we were completely stunned to discover that Mr. Peanut was black, an anglophone, and he said I'll never know what to us in his language.[197]

Quebec's largest city thus occupies an ambivalent place in relation to the entire province. On the one hand, the francophone majority is most fragile in Montreal, but on the other, it is also there that the influence and survival of the French language and Québécois culture in North America is being negotiated. In her short story "Leçon d'histoire," Proulx takes up this issue as well. Two men are debating Montreal's role as cultural capital, but cannot reach a consensus despite the conciliatory intervention

---

[195] PROULX, *AM*, 45.
[196] Ibid.
[197] Margaret ATWOOD and Victor-Lévy BEAULIEU. *Two Solicitudes: Conversations*. Toronto: McClelland & Stewart, 1998. 144-45.

of the woman seated between them. The one's Montreal is accusing, while the other is affectionately rolling the 'r':

> Montréal accapare les subsides culturels de l'État les peintres de Montréal les écrivains de Montréal les dramaturges de Montréal raflent tout l'argent institutionnel comme s'il n'existait pas de créateurs en dehors de Montréal Montréal veut tuer les régions autres que Montréal Montréal Montréal. Montrréal a besoin d'aide votre survie dépend de la survie de Montrréal toutes les régions devraient spontanément encourager et vivifier la culture à Montréal au lieu de se sentir si petitement jaloux de Montréal c'est à Montrréal que se joue le test de la survivance du fait français rien qu'à Montrréal Montrréal.[198]

Later on the discussion turns to Quebec sovereignty and hints at yet another of Montreal's liaisons, that with Toronto or (English) Canada, which will be focused on in chapter 4.5.

Strictly speaking, the image of the two solitudes has never accurately reflected the actual situation in Quebec, least so in Montreal. Not only has there been a degree of continuous mixing and interaction between the communities of respective English or French Canadian descent, but a third party has also always been involved. First of all the indigenous population has to be mentioned; and although it has practically disappeared from collective memory, present Montreal is located at the site of the former native village Hochelaga,[199] the name of which designates one of today's poorest districts of the city. Later, immigrants increasingly took on the role of the third partner in the dualistic English-French relationship and are now often referred to as the 'Other Solitudes' – a phrase originally introduced by Linda Hutcheon, co-editor of the book *Other Solitudes: Canadian Multicultural Fictions* (1990), which focuses on the immigrant experience and ethnic diversity in Canada.

The title of the short story "*Rouge et blanc*" points to the shared and interlinked history of the Amerindian and white settler populations, whose legacies – as embodied by the colours of the national flag[200] – have shaped modern Canada. At the same time *rouge* may equally alert one to the fact that the confrontations between the First and the Founding Nations in part constitute some of the bloody chapters of Canadian history.

---

[198] PROULX, *AM*, 74.
[199] Cf. Ginette MICHAUD. "De la 'Primitive Ville' à la Place Ville-Marie: lectures de quelques récits de fondation de Montréal." In *Montréal imaginaire: ville et littérature*. Eds. Gilles Marcotte and Pierre Nepveu. Montréal: Fides, 1992. 17.
[200] Yet, red and white – proclaimed as Canada's official colours in 1921 by King George V – were intended to represent France and England (cf. GOVERNMENT OF CANADA. "Elements of the Flag." 17 Nov. 2008. *Canadian Heritage*. 28 Sept. 2009 <http://www.pch.gc.ca/pgm/ceem-cced/symbl/df6-eng.cfm>). In her story, Proulx criticises the sometimes seemingly categorical exclusion, if not suppression, of the autochthonous people from the dominant national discourse.

"*Rouge et blanc*" is an atheistic prayer addressed to Aataentsic, mother of humanity, and spoken by a young *Amérindienne* from Kanahwake. Enraged by the injustices her community had to suffer, the protagonist and first person narrator attempted suicide, but now decides to tame her anger, because "*la haine ne fait pas survivre.*"[201] She subsequently chooses to stay in Montreal to infiltrate those who do not stop conquering her people. There she wants to put herself in the other's position in order to see herself through their eyes and understand how the conquerors end up condemning instead of pitying the defeated. Furthermore, she likens the oppression of the indigenous peoples resulting from white supremacy to that of French Canadians caused by anglophone supremacy: "*Je veux goûter le salé de leurs larmes, lorsqu'ils pleurent l'injustice qui leur échoit depuis cent ans et oublient la nôtre qui dure depuis des siècles.*"[202] Thus the narrator redirects their gaze and even appropriates their language: "*Je veux apprendre à parler vite et fort comme eux, en écrasant d'avance les arguments de l'autre.*"[203] Her declaration highlights the power of language not only as a bridge, reaching out to the other, but also as a weapon to silence the other. Although she appears resigned to the apparently insurmountable barrier between the conquerors and their "enemies" ("*Nos voies parallèles ont été forcées de se rencontrer, et ni eux ni nous n'en serons jamais heureux*"), it is through the mediation of Montreal and a reconciliation with the dominant culture that she manages to deal with her cultural uprootedness and to reconnect with her community ("*Quand je retournai parmi les miens, j'aurai leur force en plus de la mienne*").[204] In the end she reaches the conclusion that it is necessary to learn to put down new roots or to accept one's disappearance.

In the same way, the protagonist in "*Jaune et blanc*," a young woman from Shanghai, knows that she has to enroot herself in the new soil without forgetting where she has come from. Dedicated to the well-known migrant author Ying Chen, the story is a pastiche[205] of the latter's work, as it is overtly reminiscent of Chen's novel *Les lettres chinoises*, in which a young man emigrates from Shanghai to Montreal and recounts the culture shocks and difficulties he encounters in his chosen exile.

---

[201] PROULX, *AM*, 194.
[202] PROULX, *AM*, 195.
[203] Ibid.
[204] PROULX, *AM*, 194-95.
[205] Cf. Gilles DUPUIS. "Transculturalism and *écritures migrantes*." In *History of Literature in Canada: English-Canadian and French-Canadian*. Ed. Reingard M. Nischik. Rochester: Camden House, 2008. 508. See also SHIRINIAN, 15.

In Proulx's short story, the narrator sends a letter to her grandmother in China to reflect on her life in Montreal, especially its initial phase when she was still *"un arbuste chinois fraîchement transplanté en Amérique du Nord."*[206]

The protagonist's initiation to Montreal takes place in a large store with a strange name, as she says, that gives no indication of its contents: "Canadian Tire." Similar to the narrator of *"Gris et blanc,"* who compares the city's stores to villages – mercantile microcosms of a capitalist society, so to say – the woman is intimidated by a place (and culture) where objects seem to have taken precedence over human beings. The reason why she goes to this store was to find a stake to support the dahlias that she has planted in the garden of her new landlord; thus the metaphor of planting one's roots is elaborated. According to flower symbolism, dahlias are not only a symbol of dignity but also of the discovery of the New World.[207] Therefore they are an apt symbol to illustrate the narrator's situation. Immigrants are often faced with uprootedness and alienation as a direct consequence of their migration, and for some it means a struggle to keep intact their sense of dignity. While the heroine of *"Jaune et blanc"* has already planted her flowers, the fact that she does not do so in her own garden and that she is looking for support implies that she has not yet been fully integrated.

It is into a peculiar sociolinguistic environment that the character has to tune herself. At first, when she is completely lost in the store, she fears that "the codes" for this new life will forever escape her: *"Je n'ai jamais connu d'angoisse plus grande qu'à ce moment-là, grand-mère, à ce moment où Montréal m'est apparu comme une énigme indéchiffrable dont les clés et les codes pour survivre m'échapperaient à jamais."*[208] Additionally, when a man approaches to help her in her distress, he immediately excludes her from the linguistic/cultural majority by addressing her in French-accented English. Perhaps contrary to the reader's expectation, the woman replies in French, the only North American language she knows, as she remarks:

> Je lui ai répondu en français, qui est la seule langue d'Amérique du Nord que je connaisse, mais aucune langue à cet instant n'avait d'utilité pour décrire un objet dont j'ignorais le nom, et lorsque je lui ai dit avec affolement « non merci », il a interprété malheureusement

---

[206] PROULX, *AM*, 55.
[207] Cf. Jonathan RADFORD. "The Dahlia in Italy." *Life in Italy*. 28 Sept. 2009 <http://www.lifeinitaly.com/garden/dahlia-italy.asp>. Kathleen KARLSEN. "Flower Symbolism Guide." *Living Arts Originals*. 13 Sept. 2009. Living Arts Enterprises LLC. 28 Sept. 2009 <http://www.livingartsoriginals.com/infoflowersymbolism.htm>.
[208] PROULX, *AM*, 54.

ces mots comme une invitation à m'abandonner sur-le-champ, au lieu d'y voir une formule préliminaire de politesse et un appel au secours.[209]

Obviously the misunderstanding is not a question of language – neither French nor English can help her in this case – but of communication, that is, of miscommunication, as the man fails to respond to her non-verbal call for help, because he takes her "*non merci*" literally. In the end, and three hours later, she leaves the store with a mind bending under its weight and with empty hands.

After this disillusionment, and even though there was nobody to point her towards the right direction, the protagonist immerses herself in her new environment. Since then, she tells her grandmother, the St. Lawrence has become as familiar to her as the Huangpu and (super-) abundance has likewise become part of her daily life and no longer frightens her: "*Le foisonnement, maintenant, ne me fait plus peur, et le trop-plein et le vide fatalement se rejoignent.*"[210] She speaks about her newly acquired freedom in ambiguous terms, because her autonomy denotes on the one hand solitude and loneliness, but on the other self-confidence and independence ("*Ce n'est pas facile de comprendre tout à coup ce qu'est la liberté, la douloureuse et magnifique liberté*").[211] At the same time the young woman acknowledges that China has also changed and speculates whether one day there will no longer be any difference between being Chinese and being North American.

For the moment she has found a place, which allows her to move forward, while maintaining ties to her origins: "*J'ai trouvé mon lieu, grand-mère, celui au centre de moi qui donne la solidité pour avancer, j'ai trouvé mon milieu.*"[212] By saying that she has found her "middle," the narrator evokes China, the so-called 'middle country' or 'middle kingdom,' and suggests that she has resolved her identity fractures in Montreal, but continues to be her Chinese self. After all, roots are portable, as Neil Bissoondath argues:

> My own roots are portable, adaptable, the source of a personal freedom that allows me to feel 'at home' in a variety of places and languages without ever forgetting who I am or what brought me here. My roots travel with me, in my pocket, as it were, there to guide or succour me as need be. They are, in the end, the sum of my experience, historical, familial and personal. They are, in the end, my sense of self.[213]

---

[209] Ibid.
[210] PROULX, *AM*, 56.
[211] PROULX, *AM*, 57.
[212] Ibid.
[213] BISSOONDATH (1994), 26.

Moreover, critical conceptions of home are neither homogenous or static nor limited to a mere physical or geographic place, but allow for multiple localities and dimensions.[214] 'Home' is a place where personal, cultural and social meaning is grounded:

> [N]otions of 'home' include not only territorial attachment, but also adherence to transportable cultural ideas and values. Often a great sense of belonging to a specific place is accompanied by the wish to reproduce and/or reinvent 'traditions' and 'cultures' associated with 'home.' It is not only national, cultural and social belongings, but also a sense of self, of one's 'identity,' which corresponds to various conceptualizations of home.[215]

However, the protagonist's sense of feeling at home in Montreal is impeded precisely by those she seeks to mingle with.

Despite her ongoing cultural and linguistic integration, the woman feels the mistrust of the host society, in whose language battle she naturally participates. Her experience in the Canadian Tire store reflects the linguistic imbroglio of a city where languages are in permanent friction:

> Dans ce magasin où un francophone s'est adressé à moi en anglais, il y avait aussi le reflet de ce terrain mouvant où se côtoient les langues d'ici, le reflet de ce combat très courtois que les francophones de Montréal rêvent de remporter sans combattre. Je parle mieux français chaque jour, mais chaque jour, je sens leur méfiance. Je reste une ombre légère en retrait. Ils sont les seuls à pouvoir se libérer de leur méfiance, les seuls à pouvoir conquérir le sol qui leur appartient déjà.[216]

She rightly points out that it is not up to her to liberate Montreal's Francophones from their mistrust, implying that integration is a two-way process, to which she has been contributing her due.

Slightly more radical is the approach adopted by the Italo-Québécois "I" narrator – *"une femme de dix-huit ans orpheline du passé et québécoise,"*[217] according to her self-description – in *"Rose et blanc."* In this homage to Marco Micone, the narra-

---

[214] Deborah Keahey expounds on the multi-dimensional and interconnected layers of meaning of 'home': "To be at home in a *physical* sense may involve feelings of safety, of being comfortable and relaxed in your own body, and in the body's material surroundings. Being at home *psychologically* may involve an acceptance of who you are, and a sense of inner peace with yourself. The *social* dimension of being at home may involve the feeling of being part of a larger community, of having a role to play within human networks of family, friends, lovers, and colleagues, while the *spiritual* dimension might involve a feeling of harmony with nature, or of having a belief and value system that gives order and meaning to your life. Finally, being at home in an *intellectual* sense may involve knowing and understanding the world around you, or some part of it, and being able to control, shape, and transmit ideas." (Deborah KEAHEY. *Making It Home: Place in Canadian Prairie Literature*. Winnipeg: U of Manitoba P, 1998. ix-x; *my italics*).

[215] Nadje AL-ALI and Khalid KOSER. "Transnationalism, International Migration and Home." In *New Approaches to Migration? Transnational Communities and the Transformation of Home*. Eds. Nadje Al-Ali and Khalid Koser. London: Routledge, 2002. 7.

[216] PROULX, *AM*, 56.

[217] PROULX, *AM*, 98.

tor declares that she has enough of being an immigrant and that she will be "*plus francophone que les francophones de souche.*"[218] In his article "Citizenship, Language, and Modernity" Iain Chambers suggests the following:

> If it is language rather than the localized familiarities of a circumscribed territory that provides us with a home [...], then a sense of abode, of being at home, occurs in a more transitory but also more resilient structure than that proposed in the inherited genealogies of blood and soil. [...] And if language is our home, it is also a home for others.[219]

Thus the narrator's various languages seem to provide her with a multi-located home, but as she wants to claim the country as her own, she blends in with the dominant majority. In the excerpt below the character explains how her decision has resulted in a rupture with her parents:

> Mes parents me parlent anglais depuis que je suis née, anglais et italien pour me garder immobile, cramponnée à nos familles de Saint-Léonard et au rêve américain, mes parents me souhaiteraient agenouillée jusqu'à ma mort devant les lampions d'un pays révolu. Je suis née ici, je ne suis pas une immigrante, je veux occuper le territoire. Depuis que je sais que ce coin de terre est francophone, je refuse de m'extraire de la majorité dominante, je refuse de stagner dans les rangs des exclus, je refuse de parler anglais avec mes parents. La guerre a éclaté depuis entre nous, [...] et je dois m'éloigner d'eux pour apprendre à livrer ce combat ridicule [...].[220]

By linguistic means her parents have striven to keep their daughter tied to her Italian roots and to impose their version of the American Dream on her. As a consequence the narrator deems it necessary to distance herself from her background to learn how to fight "this ridiculous battle," as she calls it, which probably refers to the paradox that she has to struggle to feel at home in the country of her birth.

How many more times will they be required to justify their existence, the narrator wonders in the anonymous love letter (*"je suis la femme de ta vie"*)[221] she is writing to her Italian professor, Ugo Lagorio. Sometimes she rails against her *"italianité"* – *"Je ne sais pas ce que me veut ce fantôme irritant, moi qui ne suis jamais allée en Italie et qui a toujours détesté les pâtes"*[222] – but the more she disclaims it, the more it keeps haunting her. Yet, her declaration of love to Ugo Lagorio is at the same time one to her origins. After all, they cannot help that the memory of figs[223] is in their blood, in contrast to the cold and sour winter apples of people born here, the woman explains. This is one of several contradictions about the protagonist, who, at

---

[218] PROULX, *AM*, 96.
[219] Iain CHAMBERS. "Citizenship, Language, and Modernity." *PMLA* 117.1 (January 2002): 29-30.
[220] PROULX, *AM*, 96.
[221] PROULX, *AM*, 95.
[222] PROULX, *AM*, 97.
[223] Proulx alludes to the title of a book by Marco Micone: *Le figuier enchanté* (1992).

an earlier point, emphasised that she was likewise born *here*. Her potentially conflicting hybridity repeatedly prevents her from uniting the *here* and the *there*, and thus further complicates the process of redefining herself as a second generation immigrant in a society that is itself in perpetual transformation. This calls also for a redefinition of 'home':

> It means to conceive of dwelling as a mobile habitat, as a mode of inhabiting time and space not as though they were fixed and closed structures, but as providing the critical provocation of an opening whose questioning presence reverberates in the movement of the languages that constitute our sense of identity, place and belonging. There is no one place, language or tradition that can claim this role. [...] So, *I* finally come to experience the violence of alterity, of other worlds, languages and identities, and there finally discover my dwelling to be sustained across encounters, dialogues and clashes with other histories, other places, other people.[224]

The diaspora experience in particular, especially in a highly cosmopolitan context like that of Montreal, is nourished by the encounter with alterity. Hall affirms, "Diaspora identities are those which are constantly producing and reproducing themselves anew, through transformation and difference."[225]

4.4. "Je me souviens" – *Writing Memory*

> Le passé est imparfait, toutes les grammaires le proclament.[226]

"We are who we frequent," Gail Scott quotes in her "Notes of an Anglo-Québécois Writer" and asserts, "Doubtless, the writer one ends up becoming, is in part, the fruit of chance encounters."[227] When Alistair Mackenzie scours the shops for a Christmas present for his daughter at the beginning of *Doing the Heart Good*, and finds boxed paper and a fountain pen "suggestive somehow of elegance and agelessness," he reconsiders that it would be wiser to keep the gift for himself to ensure the longevity of his "recollections of people who have been part of [his] life or intrusions into it."[228] On the one hand, Mackenzie admits that it is to gratify his vanity that he is writing

---

[224] Iain CHAMBERS. *Migrancy, Culture, Identity*. London and New York: Routledge, 1994. 4.
[225] Stuart HALL. "Cultural Identity and Diaspora." In *Colonial Discourse and Post-colonial Theory: A Reader*. Eds. Patrick Williams and Laura Chrisman. NY: Columbia UP, 1994. 402.
[226] Statement by the narrator in PROULX (1993), 32.
[227] SCOTT, 6.
[228] BISSOONDATH, *DHG*, 13-14, 18.

down these stories, which are for the most part the products of chance encounters in his life. On the other, this sudden urge towards the end of his life to give his memories a more durable form reveals "a desperate attempt to survive his death";[229] his "scribblings" are an antidote to being forgotten:

> Nothingness, non-existence, does not frighten me. What does disturb me is falling into a void *in this world*. Turning to nothing *in this world*. Fading within a generation or two to just a name and a few photographs. The thought of such obscurity causes my heart to thunder. It coats my insides in ice. For only in the memory of this world is there an afterlife.
>
> It's because of this – fear of it, resistance to it – that I've recently taken to jotting down some of the episodes of my life. [...] As my writer friend might have said, I scribble, therefore I am, and perhaps, later, I still shall be.[230]

Moreover, he would like to bequeath his autobiographical narrative to his grandson François so that, one day, he may have a deeper understanding of his family background and so that he himself may establish a lasting bond to his grandson, to whom he feels alienated to some extent. Mackenzie ponders on his memoirs:

> I would like my grandson to have them one day, they may prove of some interest to him as he reaches that inevitable point in his life where a grasp of the larger family picture acquires a certain urgency, but I worry that they might end up a mere curiosity in his hands, some kind of exotic bauble, undecipherable cyphers whose flavours and subtleties would prove forever inaccessible because of what is already, to him, the passive, second-hand language in which they are written.[231]

In the end, however, the narrator puts this pessimism into perspective, as he foresees a joint future for himself and his francophone grandson despite their language difference.

The novel's preoccupation with the past and memory is evident from the very outset. Although the first-person narrator does not care much about chronological order, Mackenzie begins the review of his life with the year of his birth (as related to him by his mother). In a series of fourteen paragraphs nearly each one starts with "In the year of my birth," "In that year" or "That was the year [...]" – the "Year of the Forgettable,"[232] according to his sister – and juxtaposes historical and political events with trivial and sometimes hilarious personal incidents. Throughout the book individual and collective memory are thus mixed.

In the relatively recent and growing field of memory studies, the focus has shifted from the analysis and interpretation of historical facts to the issue of how and

---

[229] Bissoondath quoted in KRUK, 63.
[230] BISSOONDATH, *DHG*, 16. See also page 328, on which Mackenzie points out to his daughter the importance of narrating oneself – to oneself and to others.
[231] BISSOONDATH, *DHG*, 18.
[232] BISSOONDATH, *DHG*, 5.

by whom the past is being remembered.[233] In Mackenzie's case the act of remembering is episodic, highly subjective, of course, and liable to his occasional misjudgements, which may or may not be qualified by the intervention of Mary or another character. Even if the narrator's remembering serves Bissoondath as a tool to represent and discuss historical developments in Quebec of mainly the second half of the twentieth century, Mackenzie's stories should not be confused with historiographical accounts. Kristina Rödder explains the magic of the "treacherous territory of memory"[234] and how it deviates from history:

> Memory is the evocation of times past. It differs from history, yet both are closely connected elements in our efforts at making sense of the world. *History*, as defined by common sense, is usually understood as something intellectual, that which is written down, which is official or agreed upon by many historians, is what is disconnected from any specific individual. *Memory*, on the contrary, is experience recalled by people, with all the distortion, faultiness, and subjectivity inherent in the process of remembering. [...] Memory can [...] help create a more comprehensive picture of the past than historical facts alone.[235]

Through the protagonist's personal recollections, of the October Crisis for instance, parts of Quebec's history are also rendered more immediate. Moreover, the interactions between individual characters in *Doing the Heart Good* exemplify some of the misunderstandings existing between their respective cultural groups, as shown in the following discussion Jacques and Mackenzie have about the events in Montreal in 1970:

> [Jacques] turned white. In a precise and raucous voice, he said, 'They were a handful of misguided souls fighting for their language. It was a matter of survival.'
> 'Their lives weren't threatened.'
> 'Their souls were.'
> I leaned forward in my chair. 'But, Jack, only one side killed.'
> He stared at me for a full minute, as if trying to puzzle out my equation. Then his eyelids flickered. A sadness shadowed his pupils. I saw that, at some fundamental level, a level perhaps to which I had no access, I had failed to grasp something essential – maybe even

---

[233] Cf. Hans-Jürgen GRABBE and Sabine SCHINDLER. "Introduction." In *The Merits of Memory: Concepts, Contexts, Debates*. Eds. Hans-Jürgen Grabbe and Sabine Schindler. Heidelberg: Winter, 2008. 1. According to Patrick H. Hutton, the "topic of memory broke suddenly into scholarly discourse during the 1980s" and has sustained interest in various fields ever since (Patrick H. HUTTON. "Memory and the Problem of Historical Identity in Our Times." In *The Merits of Memory: Concepts, Contexts, Debates*. Eds. Hans-Jürgen Grabbe and Sabine Schindler. Heidelberg: Winter, 2008. 81).
[234] BISSOONDATH, *DHG*, 22.
[235] Kristina RÖDDER. "Remembering the 'Good War': World War II, Historiography, and 'Memoriography' at the End of the 20th Century." In *The Merits of Memory: Concepts, Contexts, Debates*. Eds. Hans-Jürgen Grabbe and Sabine Schindler. Heidelberg: Winter, 2008. 263.

had understood nothing in the entire drama, now so many years later merely an episode in history.[236]

It is one of those rare moments in which the narrator admits his own ignorance and concedes that the many years have not necessarily made him wise. He elaborates on his and his francophone son-in-law's divergent views of history:

> Jack and I, jealous of our irreconcilable versions of the same story, were like blind men who knew a great deal but who understood little. […] I saw that people live constantly with contradiction, I saw that we are all the time intimate with the irreconcilable. And I saw too that Jack and I cannot either of us be trusted to excavate truth from the past. I resolved never again to talk with Jack about the things that divide us. I chose that night to get along with my son-in-law.[237]

To turn a blind eye to what divides them does not appear to be the ideal solution, however. In fact, such behaviour evokes again the concept of the two solitudes and limited communication, despite the good intentions that motivate Mackenzie not to broach highly charged topics any more.

Je me souviens – "I remember" – is the motto of the province of Quebec. It is not an exercise in nostalgia but draws attention to the importance of remembering the past and its lessons to make more sense of the present and help shape the future. Victor-Lévy Beaulieu affirms, "I don't think the past is preferable to the present. I do think that the present is often uninhabitable because we've forgotten the past, because we don't use it as a lever to make the present conform to our desires, needs, and dreams."[238] History and its legacies are particularly important in Quebec.[239] The evolution the country has undergone as a result of a rather tumultuous history of (francophone) conquest, defeat and reconquest (as outlined in chapter 2) imparts one of the biggest stimuli to Québécois culture in addition to the central role of the French language. Today the province's motto does not only figure on Quebecers' licence plates, but since as early as 1883 it is also engraved below Quebec's coat of arms, which was officially adopted in 1939. While the phrase *Je me souviens* was once primarily used to refer to a French Canadian lineage (at least according to popular usage), it now conjures up various memories as a more universal reminder of

Fig. 5

---

[236] BISSOONDATH, *DHG*, 143.
[237] BISSOONDATH, *DHG*, 144-45.
[238] ATWOOD and BEAULIEU, 216.
[239] Conlogue pointedly remarks, "In English Canada, history is dead and pinned to a board. In Quebec, it is alive" (CONLOGUE, 10).

Quebec history, similarly to the coat of arms. Through a tripartite structure the emblem (fig. 8), reflecting the country's political history, embodies the era of *La Nouvelle France* (three gold fleurs-de-lis on a blue background), the British regime (a blue-tongued, blue-clawed gold leopard on a red background) and the Canadian period (a triple green, gold-veined maple leaf on a gold background).[240]

Doing the Heart Good is clearly more concerned with Alistair Mackenzie's personal memory than with a national one, though the two are frequently juxtaposed. The protagonist's relationship with Tremblay, for example, paints a larger societal picture of anglophone-francophone relations in Montreal. If it were not for the Mackenzie's refusal to speak French, his own motto could indeed be *Je me souviens*. In particular, however, he remembers being "special by virtue of history"[241] – that is, he is aware of some sort of supremacy as justified by (historical) anglophone dominance. Consequently, when Mackenzie declares, after Tremblay has become his upstairs neighbour, "And so things changed. Tremblay came to live above me,"[242] there is the subtext of the changed power relations in Quebec subsequent to the Quiet Revolution. After Francophones had become *maîtres chez eux* again, a number of Anglos were not happy at all with the virtual role reversal of Anglophones and Francophones, so they would probably agree with Mackenzie's statement and its double meaning: "This living beneath Tremblay: it does my heart no good, no good at all."[243]

Not surprisingly, Alistair Mackenzie gets a lot of things simply wrong; on several occasions he evidences cultural myopia in a way not much unlike Laurel does in Proulx's "Les aurores montréales." Yet, Bissoondath's readers know that they are dealing with a narrator who is neither omniscient nor reliable. Early in the novel Mackenzie mentions the recurrent deficiencies regarding his memory. For instance, he more than once mistakes his daughter for his departed wife, and in vain does he try to cover up what was a "slip of the mind"[244] as a slip of the tongue. But the stories covering the seventy-five years of his life are not meant to give a faithful account of this time span or to "excavate truth from the past"; rather they eventually provide Mackenzie with the benefit of hindsight through narrative reflection. In his analysis

---

[240] Cf. MINISTERE DE LA JUSTICE. "Devise et armoiries du Québec." 2009. *Gouvernement du Québec*. 28 Sept. 2009 <http://www.formulaire.gouv.qc.ca/cgi/affiche_doc.cgi?dossier=655&table=0&>.
[241] BISSOONDATH, *DHG*, 345.
[242] BISSOONDATH, *DHG*, 113.
[243] BISSOONDATH, *DHG*, 299.
[244] BISSOONDATH, *DHG*, 23.

of autobiographical writing, applicable also to Mackenzie's fictional autobiography, Mark Freeman moreover reconsiders the notion of 'truth':

> [I]n relying on the vantage point of the present for their [i.e. autobiographical texts] very sense, it could be held that truth is, of necessity, out of question. But there is little reason [...] to think of truth in this limited and simplistic way. Can we not say, in fact, that the reality of living in time requires narrative reflection and that reflection, in turn, opens the way toward a more comprehensive and expansive conception of truth itself?[245]

Paul John Eakin elaborates that "the writing of autobiography is properly understood as an integral part of a lifelong process of identity formation in which acts of self-narration play a major part."[246] Thus, Mackenzie's narrative supplies a framework in which the protagonist can place himself through experiences and negotiate memory and his sense of self. Additionally, his remembering allows for an impression of continuity between the actions of the past and the present, which appears to be vital to his imagined selfhood and consistency of consciousness.[247] The process of self-narration, in short, is not only about leaving a mark, but it offers Mackenzie the possibility of understanding himself and others better.

Writing and memory are also intimately connected in several of Proulx's short stories, especially in the 'colour stories,' most of which are composed in the form of a letter. *Les Aurores montréales* begins with the narrator announcing, "*Je t'écris, Manu, même si tu ne sais pas lire.*"[248] Apart from the fact that the young immigrant from Costa Rica is addressing his dog, the opening indicates that the letter is less concerned with the transfer of information than with bridging the past and the present, memories of a life of poverty and his current experience in an affluent society. For the protagonist it seems central to link distant and recent memory in order to cope with the displacement engendered by his migration.

Remembering is of utmost importance to the young *Amérindienne* in "*Rouge et blanc*," whose decision to stay in Montreal can be read as a refusal to forget that the city is built on the land of her ancestors. In her case, the act of narrating herself takes on the form of a prayer and offers emotional and cultural catharsis. In "*Rose et blanc*," the *Italo-Québécoise*, who alternately draws on and rebels against the "memory of figs" in her blood, writes not only to express her feelings in a love letter to her

---

[245] Mark FREEMAN. *Rewriting the Self: History, Memory, Narrative.* London: Routledge, 1993. 32.
[246] Paul John EAKIN. *How Our Lives Become Stories: Making Selves.* Ithaca: Cornell UP, 1999. 101.
[247] Cf. also Nicola KING. *Memory, Narrative, Identity: Remembering the Self.* Edinburgh: Edinburgh UP, 2000. 2.
[248] PROULX, *AM*, 7.

Italian professor, but also as a statement of self-assertion in the francophone society she lives in:

> J'écris moi aussi, Ugo Lagorio. Pour l'instant, ce ne sont que des brouillons hésitants, qui se contentent de dénuder peu à peu la langue pour en chercher la moelle, mais bientôt ce sera des romans, et je serai meilleure que les meilleurs écrivains d'ici [...].[249]

Likewise, self-narration serves the narrator of "*Jaune et blanc*" rather as a means to claim her place in society than to fulfil the actual purpose of her letter – telling her dying grandmother in China about her gradual integration into Montreal life – since words between the sender and the addressee have never been necessary anyway (*"Les mots entre nous n'ont jamais été nécessaires, et ceux-ci trouveront leur chemin pour t'atteindre"*).[250] Writing in this case is thus a performative act linked with identity construction, because, as Judith Butler argued, identity does not "exist prior to [its] articulation in historically specific, and situational, discursive contexts."[251]

At one point a character in *Doing the Heart Good* exclaims, "The past! You say that as if it's gone. Poof! Disappeared into thin air. We're none of us so lucky."[252] That is precisely the downside of *Je me souviens*: one can hardly rid oneself of the sometimes burdensome heritage of the past, given that memory also includes adversity and "accumulated pain," terms, in which Quebec history is frequently conceptualised, according to Jocelyn Létourneau.[253] A rather painful memory of recent Canadian and Quebec history has been creatively translated by Proulx into a love story: "Oui or no," which Fisher describes as a *"conte postmoderne sur le référendum de 1995."*[254]

---

[249] PROULX, *AM*, 96.
[250] PROULX, *AM*, 57.
[251] Judith BUTLER. *Gender Trouble: Feminism and the Subversion of Identity*. New York: Routledge, 1990. 9. In an interview Proulx says about her own writing: "*écrire est ma façon de m'inscrire dans le monde*" (qtd. in DESMEULES).
[252] BISSOONDATH, *DHG*, 156.
[253] Cf. LETOURNEAU, 128.
[254] Dominique D. FISHER. "Transculturalité et délocalisation dans *Les aurores montréales* de Monique Proulx." In *Le Québec à l'aube du nouveau millénaire: Entre tradition et modernité*. Ed. Marie-Christine Weidmann Koop. Québec: Presses de l'Université du Québec, 2008. 313.

4.5. A Tale of Two Cities

> It was the best of times, it was the worst of times, it was the age of wisdom, it was the age of foolishness, it was the epoch of belief, it was the epoch of incredulity, it was the season of Light, it was the season of Darkness, it was the spring of hope, it was the winter of despair, we had everything before us, we had nothing before us, we were all going direct to Heaven, we were all going direct the other way [...].
>
> - Charles Dickens, *A Tale of Two Cities*[255] -

"I watch you sitting there reading *A Tale of Two Cities* as if you haven't got a care in the world,"[256] Agnes somewhat reproachfully observes to her father. The latter, an expert in nineteenth century British literature, indeed repeatedly mentions that he finds his "greatest comfort"[257] in Dickens's novel, which offers him a fictional escape into the past and into another world. Because, despite living in "a late twentieth-century Dickensian environment" himself, Mackenzie prefers to return to "Dickens's evocation of the darknesses of another age."[258] As has been mentioned before, Alistair Mackenzie often does not particularly enjoy dealing with the real world and its complexities.

Dickens's famous novel figures as an important symbol with regard to the English-French dichotomy that is at the heart of Bissoondath's novel. The two cities refer to Paris and London, the capitals of the two former colonial powers that have shaped Quebec.[259] *A Tale of Two Cities* depicts the plight and oppression of the peasantry in France during the years leading up to and following the French Revolution, and parallels the situation with life in London to highlight the social inequities there. Though of completely different dimensions, a further parallel can be drawn to the circumstances in Quebec, where the long-standing oppression of the majority population and social discrepancies between Francophones and Anglophones led to the events of the Quiet Revolution in the 1960s.

---

[255] Charles DICKENS. *A Tale of Two Cities*. 1859. Oxford: Oxford UP, 1988. 1.
[256] BISSOONDATH, *DHG*, 203.
[257] BISSOONDATH, *DHG*, 76.
[258] BISSOONDATH, *DHG*, 13, 278.
[259] Quebec's 'further capitals' should be named as well: Rome, for its historically important religious influence, and Washington, for the considerable cultural and economic impact the US has exerted, especially on Montreal.

Another climax of Quebec nationalism and francophone emancipation was reached in 1995, when Quebecers were again called upon to decide on the province's independence in a referendum, which was so grippingly close that it was not clear until the very last hour that the sovereigntist cause would be defeated. The events meant a blow for the relationship between Quebec and (English) Canada, and exacerbated some of the mutual misunderstandings embedded in both cultures. In 1876, Pierre Chauveau compared the situation of English and French Canadians to the famous double staircase of the Chateau de Chambord in Paris, which two people can climb simultaneously without seeing each other. Some scholars argue that, today, not much has changed, and that anglophone and francophone Canadians lead parallel lives largely unaware of each other, meeting only rarely "on the landing of politics."[260]

The contradictory terms in which Dickens's *A Tale of Two Cities* opens reflect the ambiguous relationship of Quebec with the rest of Canada. In "Oui or no," an allegorical story of a love affair between a woman from Montreal and a man[261] from Toronto set in 1995, Proulx likewise begins the narrative by alluding to Quebec as a place paradoxically set apart from the rest of Canada yet firmly rooted within it: "*C'est l'histoire d'une femme qui rencontre un homme sans le rencontrer vraiment [...]. C'est l'histoire aussi d'un petit pays confus encastré dans un grand pays mou.*"[262] Despite their intimate relationship, the protagonist Éliane does not "really meet," that is, does not really get to know or to understand the anglophone Nick Rosenfeld and vice versa. Similarly, at the time of the referenda most Anglo-Canadians failed to understand that Franco-Quebecers felt in any way oppressed, because the latter were denied the acknowledgment of their special status as one of the nation's two founding peoples.

"Oui or no" recounts the passionate affair between Éliane and Nick Rosenfeld, including their betrayal of Éliane's partner Philippe, whom she affectionately calls Filippo, for reasons she has forgotten. The events take place at a time that could be of momentous historic importance in Quebec: "*Le petit pays se trouve dans une période*

---

[260] Chauveau quoted in CONLOGUE, 8.

[261] In another short story ("Blanc"), francophone Quebec is also represented by a woman and anglophone Canada by a man. Perhaps Proulx makes a point about unequal power distributions here. Yet, she may equally alert to the fact that marked anglophone dominance in Quebec is a thing of the past, as Franco-Quebecers, coincidentally almost at the same time as women, have liberated themselves. Apart from that, neither of the two women in the stories is in any way subjected to their male counterparts.

[262] PROULX, *AM*, 169.

de réveil et d'asphyxie, il réclame un lit à lui pour fuir les étreintes suffocantes."[263] The metaphor of the bed is employed throughout the story to illustrate the relationship between Quebec and Canada and the former's independentist aspirations. On the one hand, a bed stands for comfort and repose; it is a shelter, a haven, a place of love and togetherness. On the other, embraces can be stifling and a bed may also connote discomfort or even betrayal, as demonstrated by Éliane, who betrays Philippe by sharing a bed with Nick Rosenfeld. On the negative side, a bed additionally evokes such things as violation, insomnia and nightmares.

Indeed, the interdependency of Quebec and the rest of Canada is ambivalent; in any case it is not all bad. Sometimes "the small country" feels quite at home in the "big country's bed":

> Parfois, [le petit pays] s'assoupit paisiblement dans le lit du grand pays mou en rêvant qu'il est chez lui. Parfois, il rêve que le grand pays mou l'enserre et l'engloutit dans ses draps marécageux et il se réveille avant de disparaître.[264]

This passage manifests one of the principal motivations underlying the province's wish for secession: fear of disappearing, that is, Quebec perceives a threat of being "swallowed up" by the Confederation and losing its cultural and linguistic distinctness in the process. In 1993, when Charles Taylor thought Canada was on the brink of breaking up, he published a series of essays entitled *Reconciling the Solitudes*, in which he wrote:

> Quebec is not just the home of some six millions plus Canadian citizens, most of whom happen to speak French; Quebec sees and understands itself as a society with an aspiration to survive and flourish in its distinctness.[265]

He went on to argue that the real fuel for Quebec nationalism was in the discourse of recognition. In the following Taylor explains what he means by 'being recognised':

> I am once more using the word in the modern sense, as correlative to the term "identity." Our identity is what defines us as human agents; it is "who" we are. The recognition I am talking about here is the acceptance of ourselves by others in our identity. We may be "recognized" in other senses – for example, as equal citizens, or rights bearers, or as being entitled to this or that service – and still be unrecognized in our identity. In other words, what is important to us in defining who we are may be quite unacknowledged, may even be condemned in the public life of our society, even though all our citizen rights are firmly guaranteed.[266]

---

[263] PROULX, *AM*, 170.
[264] PROULX, *AM*, 169.
[265] Charles TAYLOR. "Impediments to a Canadian Future." In *Reconciling the Solitudes: Essays on Canadian Federalism and Nationalism*. Ed. Guy Laforest. Montreal and Kingston: McGill-Queen's UP, 1993. 199.
[266] TAYLOR, 190.

In her short prose narrative, Proulx affirms that "the small country" has everything that makes a country, but that it seems to require something else in order to be finally allowed to "sleep in its own bed":

> Le petit pays n'a pas de papiers officiels attestant qu'il est bien un pays. Il a tout autres choses qui font un pays, mais les papiers, ça, il n'a pas. [...] Les papiers ne sont pas gratuits, il faut les payer cher, il faut consentir à des sacrifices. Alors le petit pays consulte sa population, consulte, consulte. Il demande : « Nous permettez-vous d'acheter les papiers qui vont nous permettre d'être suffisamment en règle pour nous permettre d'avoir un lit à nous ? Oui ou non. »[267]

Not only do the *"papiers officiels"* refer to a political acceptance of the small country as a sovereign state, but they also involve the recognition Taylor was invoking. In short, the small country needs its existence confirmed, since *esse est percipi*[268] – to be is to be perceived – or in the words of the German philosopher Hegel, "Self-consciousness exists in and for itself when, and by the fact that, it so exists for another; that is, it exists only in being acknowledged."[269] Moreover, the above passage from Proulx mentions that there is a price to pay for independence, implying that, in being part of the Confederation, Quebec is not wholly without advantages. Even if the outcome of the referendum had been different, Quebec would never have completely severed its ties with Canada; at the very least, an economic relationship would always have been maintained.[270]

Again, the opening lines of Dickens's *A Tale of Two Cities* happen to capture the state of affairs in Quebec at the time of the referendum in 1995, as it seems indeed true to say that "it was the spring of hope, it was the winter of despair," when Quebec wanted to go "direct the other way."[271] Yet, Proulx suggests that the period was not just one of hope and subsequent disenchantment for Quebec's Francophones, but that there were equally feelings of insecurity and indecision associated with the possibility of an eventual secession. By extending the imagery surrounding the bed, the author points out that, after all, sleeping alone can be frightening as well:

> Faut-il vraiment changer? Un lit neuf ne sera-t-il pas trop dur, trop petit, trop grand? Dormir seul n'est-il pas terrifiant? Comment s'assurer qu'on ne fera pas de cauchemars? N'existe-t-il pas des façons moins draconiennes d'échapper aux coups de pied et à

---

[267] PROULX, *AM*, 169-170.
[268] Dictum by eighteenth-century Irish philosopher Bishop Berkeley (1685-1753).
[269] Qtd. in Vincent B. LEITCH et al. Eds. *The Norton Anthology of Theory and Criticism*. New York: W.W. Norton, 2001. 627.
[270] Cf. KOLBOOM and LETOURNEAU, 35.
[271] See the opening lines of *A Tale of Two Cities* quoted at the beginning of the present chapter.

l'asphyxie? Pourquoi ne pas ramper vers le rebord du vieux matelas? Pourquoi ne pas se gaver de somnifères?[272]

Yet, even if sleeping in the "new bed" is like a leap in the dark, it appears preferable to being kicked and asphyxiated. Though the notion of asphyxiation is an extremely strong one, the idea in the end goes back to what Taylor saw as Quebec's main problem: denied recognition. In the short story it says:

> Il est écrit, dans ces journaux de l'avion édités par le grand pays, que le petit pays n'est pas un pays. Il est écrit que le petit pays n'a rien de distinctif, rien à préserver, rien à exiger. S'il change de lit, on lui rendra le sommeil impossible. [...] Oh la détresse si apparente du petit pays, qui voudrait tant être fort et sûr de lui, qui souhaiterait tellement ne plus craindre de disparaître.[273]

On a different level, Nick Rosenfeld does not fully recognise Éliane in her identity either. To begin with, Nick Rosenfeld – representing anglophone Canada in sometimes fairly obvious similes (*"Nick Rosenfeld est grand et froid comme un paysage polaire"*) – pronounces her name "Alien," *"comme le monstre de l'espace, comme l'étranger qu'ils sont l'un pour l'autre."*[274] Proulx notes that they are light-years apart and do not always understand each other. Conversation between them is perilous and unequal, because they only talk in his language, although he claims to understand hers. Furthermore, Éliane feels that she is not taken seriously; whenever she prepares terribly effective sentences, they evaporate as soon as she pronounces them ("Your accent is adorable").[275] The medium seems to take precedence over the message; but when Éliane finally manages to explain the distress his voice causes her, his reply is astounding: "Same here."[276] There is apparently a fear on both sides of not understanding the other, which is no hindrance to their passionate relationship though; perhaps the contrary is the case and they are attracted by what they do not understand.

Even though their communication is limited ("Oh Éliane. My dear. Oh you. You.")[277] and their liaison basically just sexual, Nick Rosenfeld and Éliane do have a relationship, which also allows for the possibility of love. Éliane expects a fundamental upheaval should she obey Nick Rosenfeld's relentless siren call to return to him

---

[272] PROULX, *AM*, 171.
[273] PROULX, *AM*, 174-75.
[274] PROULX, *AM*, 172-73.
[275] PROULX, *AM*, 173. That Nick Rosenfeld takes more interest in how Éliane says things than in what she says indicates that their relationship is not destined to ever go beyond the mere physical level or superficialities.
[276] Ibid.
[277] PROULX, *AM*, 170, 173. See also page 174-75.

("Are we going to let *this* die? When are you coming back to Toronto?"),[278] but develops the thought a bit further and parallels it with the relationship of Quebec and Canada:

> Que se passera-t-il s'il dit « *I love you* », mots terrifiants et cinématographiques qui débouchent sur un abîme ? Que se passera-t-il s'il ne les dit pas ? Qu'arrivera-t-il au petit pays s'il ne parvient à convaincre personne ? Il faut cesser d'avoir peur. Il faut aller voir.[279]

In *Impossible Nation: The Longing for Homeland in Canada and Quebec* (1996), Ray Conlogue describes how 100,000 Canadians said "I love you" in their manner to Quebec, when they gathered in Montreal to persuade the province to stay in Canada. After the referendum it was said that Quebecers "had been moved by [this] gesture of 'love' from the anglophone majority."

> But as the days and weeks went by, the truth gradually dawned: for the first time in history, more than half of Quebec's French-speaking population had voted to leave Canada once and for all. They had been forestalled only by the monolithic No vote of the province's English-speaking minority.
> Anger set in. The media, never much inclined to explain the francophone perspective to English Canada, hardened into a bullying tone. French Canadians were characterized as racists who could not be trusted to preserve democracy in an independent Quebec. Some argued that Montreal would have to be seized and kept by Canada in order to protect the city's anglophones. […]
> Virtually nobody seemed interested in understanding why Quebeckers felt as they did. Could this red-faced, stony-eyed Canadian people be the same one which had so recently declared its love for Quebec?[280]

Charles Taylor's declaration years before the referendum that "the dialectic of misunderstanding between the two great societies in Canada has intensified"[281] evidently proved prophetic. In a similarly confused way, Éliane does not comprehend why Nick Rosenfeld does not call her any more, why he has rejected her, until she realises that she is only one of many ("Oh Éliane. Oh Carole. Oh Teresa. My love. Oh you.");[282] she gets the impression that her presence in Nick Rosenfeld's bed is no more special than Quebec's in Canada among the other nine provinces.

While Éliane engages in an affair with Nick Rosenfeld, it is all the while with Philippe/Filippo that she has been living. Philippe is a television commentator who analyses and discusses publicly "the small country's" distinctness and legitimacy of "sleeping in a new bed." He stands for the rational defender of Quebec sovereignty,

---

[278] PROULX, *AM*, 172.
[279] PROULX, *AM*, 173.
[280] CONLOGUE, 7.
[281] TAYLOR, 196.
[282] PROULX, *AM*, 177.

whereas Filippo, the one lying beside Éliane in front of the TV, fulminates privately and symbolises how much of an emotional issue the debate on independence is. It is also Filippo rather than Philippe that she is betraying, when she goes to Toronto to become once more "*un corps vaincu.*"[283] In particular when Éliane starts to mentally translate everything into Nick Rosenfeld's language ("Pass me the butter. Give me a break. Do you agree with the law voted by the National Assembly and proclaiming a new bed? Yes or No.")[284] in order to grasp the essence of their relationship, she feels that she is betraying Filippo much more than she ever could just with Nick Rosenfeld:

> Mais traduire mentalement Filippo est une expérience difficile, qui la laisse terriblement honteuse. C'est à ce moment-là qu'elle sent qu'elle le trahit vraiment, qu'elle le trahit beaucoup plus qu'avec Nick Rosenfeld.[285]

The linguistic dimension of Éliane's unfaithfulness underlines the centrality of the French language in the independentist discourse. In this respect it is also important to bear in mind that close to a hundred per cent of non-French Canadian Quebecers voted against secession from Canada.[286] The fear of Quebec's Francophones of disappearing, however, can be taken literally, because despite effective language legislation they - at least in Montreal – feel the persistent threat of English in daily life. In the short story "*Blanc,*" for example, the narrator declares, "*Montréal était familial, Montréal était un bouge sympathique et rassurant d'où nulle crainte ne pouvait sourdre, sauf celle de l'assimilation anglaise.*"[287] Another story entitled "Dépaysement" speaks of extinction; on a vacation the story's protagonist meets some fellow francophone Quebecers, who carry an animal they call "*kipichu*" in a basket with them: "*Il rit. Il dit que le kipichu est un tyran qui n'accepte pas la solitude. Il dit aussi que les kipichus sont en voie d'extinction. « Comme notre peuple »*, *ajoute-t-il brièvement en cessant de rire.*"[288]

Where Éliane and *le petit pays* will finally sleep is resolved at the end of the story, when the outcome of the "Final Consultation" sends Éliane and Filippo into each other's arms. Proulx writes that their pain and disappointment is so violent that it could easily turn to hatred. However, even though hatred might be a consolation, it

---

[283] PROULX, *AM*, 172.
[284] PROULX, *AM*, 176.
[285] PROULX, *AM*, 177.
[286] Cf. OAKES and WARREN, 31.
[287] PROULX, *AM*, 231-32.
[288] PROULX, *AM*, 148.

does not change, let alone improve the situation that "*[l]a moitié des gens du petit pays a peur de vivre dans un lit inconnu. L'autre moitié a peur de mourir dans le vieux lit connu. Comment savoir laquelle de ces deux peurs est la plus digne?*"[289] It is indeed difficult to answer which fear is more worthy, that of living in an "unknown bed" or that of dying in the old familiar one. The wording suggests that the narrator sympathises more with the pro-sovereignty cause if one assumes that life is generally preferable to death. Yet, throughout the story the author is careful to consider other points of view. For example, despite their nearly overwhelming pain, Éliane and Filippo make an effort to understand the complex motives underlying the immigrant population's rejection of Quebec independence. Already the title of the short story indicates that the narrative is interested in various perspectives. "Oui or no" not only reflects the close link between sovereignty and the language question, the solid majority *oui* among francophone Quebecers in contrast to the virtually unanimous non-francophone no-vote, but also that there is a degree of mixing and intricacy that would not accord with oversimplifying the debate to French Quebec versus English Canada. At an early point in the story the narrator wonders whether "the small country" will be allowed its own bed ("*Oui ou non*") and later on Éliane more or less asks the same question, when in her mind she is translating everything into English ("Yes or No") in an attempt to put herself into Nick Rosenfeld's shoes. The combination of the two questions asked in the course of the narrative constitutes the title and highlights once again Quebec's and Canada's inter-connectedness at the same time as Quebec's own internal (linguistic) diversity.

"*C'est malgré tout de Nick Rosenfeld que vient la fin de l'histoire.*"[290] The day after the sovereigntists were defeated, he calls Éliane and the short story thus ends with his take on their relationship and/or the conclusion of the referendum:

> Et pendant qu'elle ne parle pas, raidie par la méfiance, il dit ces quelques mots, les plus tendres qu'elle ait entendus dans sa langue, il ne répète que ces quelques mots d'apaisement véritable. (*I'm sorry. I'm sorry.*)[291]

In line with most stories of the collection, Proulx does not finish the narrative by leaving the reader with the impression of Éliane's and Filippo's acute disappointment or Éliane's personal *chagrin* at having been rejected and deserted by Nick Rosenfeld. Instead the author once more ends on a positive note. Éliane's lover apologises to her

---

[289] PROULX, *AM*, 178.
[290] PROULX, *AM*, 178.
[291] PROULX, *AM*, 178-79.

and by doing so he shows an awareness of the pain and unhappiness he has caused her. This awareness, similar to Taylor's notion of recognition, is necessary to her, especially after having been trampled on, and seems sufficient to soothe Éliane, for whom "I'm sorry" are the most tender words she has yet heard in her lover's language. Since "Oui or no" parallels their affair all the time with the relationship between "the small country" and the big one, the apology by the anglophone Nick Rosenfeld can also be interpreted as a conciliatory gesture from Canada to demonstrate that they at least acknowledge – if not quite understand – Quebec's disappointment. This is crucial if one considers that the separatist drive was largely propelled by a lack of acknowledgment in the first place.

"Oui or no" would not appear to be a typical Proulx story if it were not for the surprise twist near the ending. This stylistic and structural idiosyncrasy is a recurrent feature in many of the short stories in *Les Aurores montréales*. There are the somewhat enigmatic, philosophical endings as in "Jouer avec un chat," "Rue Sainte-Catherine" or "Leçon d'histoire" (*"Nous allons nous asseoir devant une scène, pour imaginer un instant que la vie gagne toujours"*),[292] for instance, or the ones that culminate in a shock, such as "Le futile et l'essentiel," which ends with the revelation that the mother has cancer, or "L'enfance de l'art," where the reader discovers in the last sentence that the act of fellatio was performed by a girl who is only twelve years old. Proulx evidently enjoys playing with or subverting her readers' expectations, markedly so in "Oui or no." Throughout the story she sustains a metaphorical comparison of the love affair of the francophone Éliane and anglophone Nick Rosenfeld with the relationship between Quebec and Canada, only to deconstruct the metaphor at the end:

> Doit-on voir une relation métaphorique entre la déception amoureuse d'Éliane et la déception idéologique du petit pays? Pour ma part, je m'en méfierais comme de tout ce qui est trop facile. Certes, Nick Rosenfeld appartient au grand pays dont Éliane craint l'étreinte suffocante. Mais la vie est remplie de hasards circonstanciels, et une femme n'est pas un pays, aussi petit soit-il.[293]

On the one hand, the reader is manoeuvred into drawing parallels between the romantic and the political story so that one is alerted to the metaphorical level right from the start. At the very latest it is after the author's own suggestion that one begins to see the metaphorical relation between the different levels of the short story (in the man-

---

[292] PROULX, *AM*, 75.
[293] PROULX, *AM*, 178.

ner of "Try *not* to think of a pink elephant"[294]). On the other hand, the author rightly suggests that Quebec independentism and the referendum on sovereignty with all its ramifications are indeed very complicated matters involving numerous factors, so to reduce and compare the issue to a story of an affair and subsequent disappointment would be "*trop facile.*" Still, this final deconstruction of the interpretation that the short story constantly advances is first and foremost a stylistic decision, consistent with Proulx's preferred tone – irony – as in her tongue-in-cheek comment that "life is full of circumstantial hazards."

With Éliane being from Montreal and Nick Rosenfeld from Toronto, "Oui or no" is also a tale of Canada's two most important cities (at least historically speaking). Until about the middle of the twentieth century, Montreal had been *the* metropolis in Canada – a title it then lost to Toronto; yet, Montreal has in the meantime assumed a new role as economic and cultural metropolis of francophone Quebec and as an influential city of *La Francophonie.*[295] David McGimpsey continues to speak of Montreal and Toronto as "natural civic rivals" in an essay on English language literature from Quebec, in which he writes:

> Although the quality of literature can't be arrested in something as trivial as city affiliation, this civic rivalry is nevertheless spelled into important definitions of where the Canadian literary scene is today. Toronto, the usual destination for the expat-Montrealer […] and the cultural capital of English Canada, must be accounted for by anglophones who continue to live and write in English in Montreal. Reactively, the English Montreal literary imagination often indulges in enumerating the Subaru-driving, "Kwee-beck"-saying sins of Hogtown. Admittedly, Toronto-bashing is second only to hockey among Canadian national pastimes […]. But in Montreal arts circles, the gesture can be more strategic: in casting aside the middle-class values of Upper Canada, the differences of Quebec can be co-opted as signs of personal distance from the aesthetics of English Canadian malls ("Hey, Brampton, look at me! I'm saying depanneur!").[296]

As has been discussed before, the essential language difference gives Quebecers – indirectly also Anglo-Quebecers – a degree of cultural self-confidence and a sense of uniqueness in the North American context that anglophone Canadians usually lack. While this chapter and the discussion of the short story "Oui or no" has focused on

---

[294] George Lakoff published, in fact, a book entitled *Don't Think of an Elephant!*, in which he explains: "Every word, like *elephant*, evokes a frame, which can be an image or other kinds of knowledge […]. The word is defined relative to that frame. When we negate a frame, we evoke the frame." (George LAKOFF. *Don't Think of an Elephant! Know Your Values and Frame the Debate.* White River Junction: Chelsea Green Publishing, 2004. 3).
[295] Cf. LINTEAU, 429.
[296] David MCGIMPSEY. "A Walk in Montreal: Wayward Steps Through the Literary Politics of Contemporary English Quebec." *Essays on Canadian Writing* 71 (Fall 2000): 156.

relations between francophone Quebecers and anglophone Canadians from outside of Quebec, the next section will take a closer look at how both Francophones and Anglophones living in Montreal interact with each other. Given that Franco- and Anglo-Montrealers potentially meet on a daily basis, their relationship naturally deviates from that between Francophones in Quebec and English speakers from the rest of Canada. To begin with, already the latter's physical distance, allows francophone Quebecers to maintain their preconceived opinions about them. Ray Conlogue confirms the difference between Anglo-Canadians and Anglo-Quebecers; after having spoken of anglophone Canada's prejudices against Quebec, he argues that

> an equally narrow and mistrustful view of English Canada is entrenched in Quebec. This is not to be confused with the attitude toward "les Anglais" within Quebec, where middle-class francophones are proud of their ability to speak English and often number anglophones among their friends. Their mental block is toward the rest of Canada, which they resist visiting and where their newspapers do not post correspondents.[297]

In the following, primarily the anglophone perspective will be investigated, as the Anglo-Montrealer Alistair Mackenzie presents his accounts of his dealings with francophone fellow citizens and family members.

4.6. Strangers in the Same House

> Die Sprache ist das Haus des Seins. In ihrer Behausung wohnt der Mensch.
> - Martin Heidegger[298] -

Le langage est la maison de l'Être. Dans son abri habite l'homme.	Language is the house of Being. In its home man dwells.

Describing his relationship with his sister at one point in the narrative, Mackenzie declares, "Ruth-Ann and I lived parallel lives in the same house, siblings bordering on strangers."[299] Their situation evidences that proximity – whether physical or genealogical – does not necessarily entail intimacy. For Sherry Simon, this is one of the paradoxes of urban space, where individuals can be in contact without having to in-

---

[297] CONLOGUE, 7-8.
[298] Qtd. in Christoph DEMMERLING. "Hermeneutik der Alltäglichkeit und In-der-Welt-sein (§§ 25-38)." In *Martin Heidegger, Sein und Zeit*. Ed. Thomas Rentsch. Berlin: Akademie Verlag, 2001. 108.
[299] BISSOONDATH, *DHG*, 61.

teract with one another.[300] It is after all this aspect of Montreal's urbanity that allows the protagonist of *Doing the Heart Good* to live in Quebec society without ever bothering to acquire some competence in the French language. In fact, Mackenzie behaves as if the mere idea of learning the language of the majority is ludicrous; as in the following, when he says about his wife: "She was always busy – volunteering daily at a soup kitchen, attending plays, raising funds for medical research, learning French, of all things."[301] However, his categorically anti-French outlook has to be qualified, because it is partly put on, as will be discussed, among other things, in the following.

If one regards Montreal as a house, then its inhabitants are in great numbers strangers to each other as well. Yet, as Heidegger suggested, it is in language, rather than in a physical place, that individuals live. In one of the scarce instances of enlightenment he has, Mackenzie realises the following about his son-in-law: "His language is to him as my language is to me. Denied it, he would feel bereft, unanchored, without a place where his soul could find unconditional security."[302] Does the idea of language as "the house of Being" hence support the notion of the two solitudes, of two linguistic communities living like strangers in the same city? No, it does not have to at all. First of all, there is always the possibility of leaving one's 'house,' especially in a cosmopolitan context like Montreal, whose citizens regularly engage in cross-cultural and -linguistic communication. Second, "the house of Being" does not have to be limited to a single idiom. This study has repeatedly stressed Montreal's polyglot sensibility and its high percentage of bi- or trilingual speakers. For them, it is quite natural to be at home in more than one language and to switch easily from one to the other, which brings back to mind Chambers' proposal "to conceive of dwelling as a mobile habitat."

Mackenzie and his francophone neighbour Gaston Tremblay are nevertheless literally strangers in the same house. At least from Mackenzie's point of view, their overall tense relationship is emblematic of the English-French cleavage in Quebec. One can already tell by their names that the two characters are meant to be representative of the linguistic group they belong to. The name Mackenzie is of Scottish origin and has a long tradition in Canada, where it is a relatively frequent family name. In theory, Alistair Mackenzie may thus be a descendant of such prominent Canadian

---

[300] Cf. Sherry SIMON. *Hybridité culturelle*. Montréal: L'île de la tortue, 1999. 30.
[301] BISSOONDATH, *DHG*, 74.
[302] BISSOONDATH, *DHG*, 146.

figures as Sir Alexander Mackenzie,[303] a Scottish fur trader who explored the Canadian northwest in the late eighteenth century and after whom a river and mountains are named in the Northwest Territories,[304] William Lyon Mackenzie or William Lyon Mackenzie King. The latter two are grandfather and grandson; the grandfather was the first mayor of Toronto (1834), while the grandson, commonly known as Mackenzie King, held the post of prime minister for almost twenty-two years between the 1920s and 40s, agitated for Canadian autonomy from the British government and did not speak French.[305] Alistair Mackenzie has inherited not only his last name from these powerful anglophone Canadians, but also a sense of importance and an awareness that, as he puts it, he "came from among the winners."[306] Who are the losers, then? "[O]thers, like Tremblay,"[307] he implies. Tremblay[308] is, in fact, the most common surname in Quebec, and Mackenzie's imagined superiority over his francophone neighbour extends to all of "Tremblay's people," that is, to Francophones in Quebec in general. Sometimes Mackenzie seems quite unaware of the fact – or simply ignores it for convenience's sake – that almost exclusively anglophone dominance (economically, not politically speaking) in Quebec ceased about half a century ago.

> Tremblay? [...] Some neighbours exercise a polite discretion. Others want to be chummy, with neighbourhood barbecues dancing in their heads. And then there are those like Tremblay, who lived with his wife in the duplex above ours. The fellow was the cause of constant aggravation to me. Always insisting on calling me miss-your.[309]

Most of the time, the affable Tremblay is presented as an unwanted intrusion into Mackenzie's life. Yet, by the end of the narrative it becomes clear that their quarrels are just superficial and that they may even be quite fond of one another, although neither would openly own to that. An illustrative example to introduce Mackenzie's rela-

---

[303] Cf. Laura NEILSON BONIKOWSKY. "Alexander Mackenzie, Explorer." *The Canadian Encyclopedia*. 2009. Historica Foundation of Canada. 20 Oct. 2009 <http://www.thecanadianencyclopedia.com/index.cfm?PgNm=ArchivedFeatures&Params=A261>.

[304] Cf. John EVERETT-HEATH. "Mackenzie." *Concise Dictionary of World Place-Names*. Oxford University Press. 2005. *Encyclopedia.com*. 20 Oct. 2009 <http://www.encyclopedia.com/doc/1O209-Mackenzie.html>.

[305] Cf. Victor L. RUSSELL. "Mackenzie, William Lyon." *The Canadian Encyclopedia*. 2009. Historica Foundation of Canada. 20 Oct. 2009 <http://www.thecanadianencyclopedia.com/ index.cfm?PgNm=TCE&Params=A1ARTA0004947>. See also: *Tabous sur l'histoire du Québec*. Dir. Didier DELESKIEWICZ. La Sept/Arte, 2000.

[306] BISSOONDATH, *DHG*, 344-45.

[307] BISSOONDATH, *DHG*, 344.

[308] Cf. *L'Association des Familles Tremblay*. 2009. Le Centre de généalogie francophone d'Amérique. 20 Oct. 2009 <http://www.genealogie.org/famille/tremblay/>.

[309] BISSOONDATH, *DHG*, 176.

tionship with his francophone upstairs neighbour is given by Tremblay's story of his wife's "ubiquitous breast" and Mackenzie's reaction to it:

> 'Ey, M'sieur Mackenzie –'
> I let it pass.
> '– you know, everywhere I go in t'e house, I find my wife's breast. Go to the bathroom, t'ere it is on the toilet tank. Go to the kitchen, t'ere it is on top of the *frigidaire*. One day, I find it in t'e fruit bowl, right on top of t'e bananas. You can imagine what t'at is like, you? Finding your wife's breast everywhere you go?'
> I had, to put it mildly, no answer to the question. I didn't know what to do with this crazed version of Gogol's 'The Nose'. The best I could do after a few laboured steps was mumble, 'No, I couldn't possibly.'[310]

After they have arrived at their respective doors, Mackenzie hurries inside "like a man pursued" and tells Mary the tale of Tremblay's wife's "wayward breast." "The man must be off his rocker," he adds.[311] His wife, after an initial outburst of mirth, elucidates him on the mystery: Tremblay's wife had a mastectomy years ago and her husband was referring to her prosthesis. For once, Mackenzie cannot help but admit the following:

> So convinced had I been that I was being treated to the ravings of a madman determined to discombobulate me, so intent was I on fleeing his clutches, that I had only half listened to him. I had merely dismissed the absurdity of it all. I hadn't for a moment sought to make sense of his words.[312]

This incident demonstrates that Mackenzie does not really listen to or care to understand Tremblay. On the contrary, he has his mind already made up and instinctively dismisses everything that might force him to modify his preconceived opinions. Moreover, to regard Tremblay as a rational, good-humoured individual would not agree with the role he has assigned unto his neighbour. Tremblay is cast as the French-speaking antagonist of *Monsieur* Mackenzie ("'*Mister* Mackenzie to you!' […] 'You know I won't take that *miss-your* shit from you, Tremblay'").[313] Apart from that, his inoffensive neighbour serves him as a scapegoat, in particular when he is reminded of his own faults and foolishness by his wife Mary, against whom it is hard to bear a grudge. In such cases, Tremblay "was, truth to tell, simply the convenient recipient for my outrage. Why lay blame at home when he was available?,"[314] Mackenzie confesses.

---

[310] BISSOONDATH, *DHG*, 177.
[311] BISSOONDATH, *DHG*, 178.
[312] Ibid.
[313] BISSOONDATH, *DHG*, 298.
[314] BISSOONDATH, *DHG*, 179.

There is no reason to believe that Mackenzie dislikes Tremblay as an individual. His behaviour towards him is just part of his anti-French principle and indicative of what Conlogue calls an "imperious mindset." Shortly after the 1995 referendum Conlogue writes:

> Some of the anti-French bigotry of the past has disappeared, but the older generation – which is still setting the terms of political debate, and whose voice carries across Canada – has not lost the imperious mind-set of an earlier day. Television news announcers pointedly anglicize French names ("Today, Jack Pair-ee-zo met with Loosien Boo-shard..."). A reader of the Montreal *Gazette*, deafened by the daily anti-separatist perorations on the editorial page, combs the rest of the paper for the tiniest references to the city's vibrant French cultural life.[315]

The anglicisation of French words, for example, is also a typical Alistair Mackenzie mannerism. His constant mock indignation at being addressed as "*miss-your*" is just in line with his pretended ignorance and complete disinterest in the French language and Franco-Québécois culture. Furthermore, this acting as if he had been affronted works as a means to conceal a weakness of his own. Though rarely sincere about it, the narrator is conscious that his extremely limited knowledge of French does encumber him, since it excludes him from communication several times. For the self-important literature professor, his inability to participate in or follow certain conversations is no inconsiderable inconvenience and that is why he prefers to blame others, like Tremblay, towards whom he can more easily channel his frustrations at his own deficiency. Apart from that, Mackenzie's permanent grumbling and depreciation of Francophones has become a game as well. The ludic aspect of his 'mistreatment' of his francophone neighbour manifests itself in the following passage, when Mackenzie complains about Tremblay's fleur-de-lis flag:

> 'Father,' Agnes says, 'the ceiling of your porch is his floor. He can do whatever he likes.'
> 'He's blocking my view.'
> 'Don't be absurd. Maybe if you were ten feet tall...' She laughs, disarming me enough that I join in her laughter. The fact is, I don't really care, not even for the principle. The truth is this: if I react to certain situations in certain ways, it is because this is what is expected of me. Playing the game has become a kind of reflex, but sustaining it presents a greater challenge. [...] So I gaze steadily at Tremblay's flag and perform a luxurious shrug.[316]

Subsequent to this avowal, the novel's central turning point takes place, when Mackenzie is nearly burnt in his bed and saved by Tremblay, whose flag has been set on fire. These events take place on June 24 – *Saint Jean Baptiste* Day – which is *La*

---

[315] CONLOGUE, 10-11.
[316] BISSOONDATH, *DHG*, 311-12.

Fête nationale du Québec. Some critics have reproached the novel for making its points too bluntly: "the overly obvious symbolic event brings about *rapprochement* between Mackenzie and his neighbour, Monsieur Tremblay, but the incident seems forced."[317] Mackenzie's and Tremblay's eventual *rapprochement* will be more closely examined in the next chapter.

It is easy for Mackenzie to denigrate his francophone neighbour, with whom he has always resisted becoming more intimately acquainted. To keep Tremblay, metaphorically speaking, below him not only gratifies his anglophone, smug self, but it also allows him to maintain his fantasy version of anglophone-francophone power relations. Things look different with his francophone son-in-law, because he is family and Mackenzie inevitably has to deal with him as an individual – at the very latest when they come to live together in the same household. However, given that his *weltanschauung* cannot accommodate Francophones as equal citizens for the most part, Mackenzie simply transforms Jacques into Jack. After their first meeting the following dialogue takes place between Mackenzie and his wife: "'Oh God, his name's not *Jack*, is it…' Mary shook her head. 'No, dear. It's Jacques.' Then she added, significantly, 'Jacques. Get used to it.' But he's remained Jack to me."[318] By eclipsing Jacques's francophone identity – which is possible because Jacques/Jack speaks impeccable English – and thus redefining him in accordance with his anti-French stance, his principles are not upset and Mackenzie can continue to look down on Franco-Quebecers from his imaginary heights. Yet, however comfortable it is to hide behind his prejudices, the protagonist sometimes cannot help but confess the true motivations that underlie his behaviour, as when he declines his daughter's invitation to a barbecue:

> 'You don't like Jacques's family, right?'
> 'Don't be silly, Agnes. They're fine people. A touch rustic perhaps, but one can't hold that against them. The fact is, though, that communication is a bit of a chore.'
> 'Now who's being silly. You don't speak their language and they don't speak yours. There's no communication, so where's the chore?' The tension in her voice has mounted a notch or two, and I see that I am justified in not having raised with her this very conundrum as regards my grandson.
> 'But that's precisely it, Agnes. Sitting in the midst of a party unable to participate, sitting there excluded – it's the most difficult thing in the world.'[319]

---

[317] Katherine MILLER. "Rewriting Identity." *Canadian Literature* 177 (Summer 2003): 167.
[318] BISSOONDATH, *DHG*, 8.
[319] BISSOONDATH, *DHG*, 310.

In this instance Mackenzie's unease at the prospect of feeling like a stranger at a family party becomes evident. Even more distressing, though, is the question to what extent he will be a stranger to his grandson and vice versa due to the language barrier.

Before his home was destroyed by arson, the narrator obstinately refused to contemplate moving in with his daughter. The latter never knew in how far language-related anxiety was at the bottom of her father's vehement resistance. Mackenzie writes:

> And she would think me petty were I to mention my reservations about living in a house in which my language is infrequently spoken and where cultural references are lifted from a world unknown to me. Yes, Jacques speaks fluent English, and he accepts with good humour my calling him Jack. But it is little François who causes me more than a modicum of distress. At six years of age, he has already acquired a remarkable body of language – a language I am not versed in, there never having been any need. Although he regularly watches *Sesame Street* […] and so understands much English, his refusal to speak it erects an inevitable barrier to our communication. Agnes assures me this will change as he grows older, but for the moment I find the situation difficult – not being able to converse with my grandson, I mean.[320]

Again, his comment that there has never been any need to learn French illustrates the protagonist's narrow-mindedness. In some respects, Mackenzie is practically like his six-year-old grandson – both refusing to speak the other's language. Only when forced to deal with the Other, Mackenzie might be induced to modify his rigid views. Similarly, it is only through the repeated encounters with Jacques/Jack as a consequence of their living together that they gradually cease to be strangers and that Mackenzie learns a vital truth about his son-in-law and about language in general. One night Mackenzie begins to understand an individual's indispensable personal attachment to his or her language and the "therapeutics of words,"[321] as he puts it, when he catches Jacques/Jack reading, his lips moving silently. At first, as usual, he misjudges the situation and thinks that Jacques/Jack might be dyslexic, before it dawns on him that his son-in-law is so intensely involved with what he is reading that he has to form the words also with his lips in order to savour them completely. Mackenzie speaks of a "moment of enlightenment," when he happened upon Jacques/Jack being thus engrossed in a volume of French-language poetry:

> Nothing Jack said or did could have given me a more *intuitive* grasp […] of the unfathomable fervour his language inspires in him. Other languages – English, Spanish, enough German to get by – are tools of his profession. But *his* language, that of the book, that of

---

[320] BISSOONDATH, *DHG*, 308.
[321] BISSOONDATH, *DHG*, 115.

first endearments and early scoldings, the language that speaks to him beyond meaning, in which he dreams, is the language of his very breath.[322]

This insight by a member of Montreal's anglophone community suggests a more sympathetic attitude towards the city's Francophones and their preoccupation with language; in particular if one takes into account that the incident is symbolically set in 1995, the year in which the vast majority of the province's Francophones voted for secession. As a consequence of the knowledge he has lately gained, Mackenzie may no longer dismiss the Francophones' passion and fervour about language as some form of Fascism or linguistic fundamentalism. Perhaps he will even take an interest in why Francophones feel so insecure about the status of their language in Montreal and why newspapers regularly worry about the future and survival of French or the threat of bilingualism.[323] This study has already highlighted repeatedly that the francophone majority is fragile in Montreal despite protective language legislation as outlined in chapter 2.2. A further discussion of the extent to which linguistic apprehension is well justified is beyond the scope of this study. Proulx implies that the chronic insecurity complex is not only entrenched in Québécois culture, but also that to take part in Montreal's language wars has become a reflex for some. In "Sans domicile fixe," for instance, two literature professors play at growing indignant over causes that are worth it, such as language:

> Nous jouons souvent tous les deux à nous indigner pour des causes qui en valent la peine, le Québec, la langue, le multiculturalisme menaçant, et cela nous apporte une sorte de répit heureux, un relent d'extrême jeunesse. La plupart du temps, notre indignation est factice, épuisée.[324]

While their game affords them some happy respite, they cannot enjoy it most of the time, probably because a real concern underlies their playful indignation.

It took Mackenzie virtually all his life to grasp the importance of language and that one's very reality is constructed through words. Moreover, he argues that it was

---

[322] BISSOONDATH, *DHG*, 145.

[323] It is no exaggeration to state that anxiety about the French language comes up at regular intervals in Quebec headlines. Random examples include "*Bilinguisme > nécessité ou péril?*," "*Luc Plamondon reproche aux politiciens de ne pas défendre la langue française*," "Parti Québécois seeks to affirm supremacy of French" or "*Les francophones laissent Montréal s'angliciser*" (Christian DUFOUR and Christine FRÉCHETTE. "Bilinguisme > nécessité ou péril?" *La Presse* 2 April 2009. Jocelyne RICHER. "Luc Plamondon reproche aux politiciens de ne pas défendre la langue française." *Le Soleil* 7 May 2009. "Parti Québécois seeks to affirm supremacy of French." *The Gazette* 8 June 2009. Patrick POISSON. "Les francophones laissent Montréal s'angliciser." *La Presse* 26 Oct. 2009). See also the Quebec independentist website www.vigile.net, whose columns include 'language' and 'sovereignty.'

[324] PROULX, *AM*, 223.

"History" that prevented him from ever considering the francophone perspective. After witnessing his son-in-law's absorption in his book, the narrator ponders:

> I wondered how it was that History – that big, crushing H – had blinded us to this simple truth. I found myself wishing, for the first time without resentment, that Jack could find it in himself to appreciate my attachment to *my* language, which is for me, as his is for him, a kind of lifeblood, living and vital and pulsing with possibility. But it has taken me over seventy years to understand this – and my language is to him the way German is to me: made ugly by History. He can speak it, but he cannot revel in it.[325]

In a pertinent comparison, the WWII-veteran acknowledges that for most Francophones English is a language far from neutral, since French Canadians lived for centuries with the consciousness of a *peuple vaincu* under Anglophones. Yet, Francophones and Anglophones do not have to be eternally haunted by history; "we must not become prisoners of the past," Bissoondath exhorts in an interview.

> We must remember that the present and the future are still to be made. Our personal and cultural pasts were shaped by certain specific contexts. Is it sensible to shape today's self by yesterday's context? The world evolves. Societies evolve. So must we as individuals.[326]

In *Doing the Heart Good* hope is pinned on the new (bilingual) generation as personified by François:

> I wonder whether he, my daughter's son, repository of that whole other stream of unreconcilable history, will escape the bonds and barbs that encumber his father and his grandfather. I wonder whether he will be free to revel in the beauty that lies beyond our truths.[327]

4.7. Between Humility and Epiphany

> Monstrueuse est l'Histoire et monstrueux le politique, monstrueux sont les maîtres d'un monde qui ne voit pas l'amour.
>
> - Proulx, "Leçon d'histoire"[328] -

The texts by Bissoondath and Proulx under investigation in the present study share several thematic, stylistic and structural similarities. For example, Proulx's sudden twists at the end of her stories can be compared to the turning points in Mackenzie's episodic narrative. Each of his encounters, or rather confrontations, with other people

---

[325] BISSOONDATH, *DHG*, 146.
[326] Bissoondath cited in SANKAR, 48.
[327] BISSOONDATH, *DHG*, 147.
[328] PROULX, *AM*, 75.

occasions a transformation in his life and usually leaves the protagonist of *Doing the Heart Good* a little wiser (or sometimes not). Although the seventy-five-year-old literature professor talks of wisdom as "the gift of the years,"[329] the seventy-five years of his life have not necessarily made him wise. At one point Mackenzie concedes, "I searched my storehouse of wisdom and found it meagre. History and decades, I understood, have not disarmed my helplessness."[330] Neither Bissoondath's nor Proulx's works are didactic, yet both clearly seek to promote a rapprochement between Montreal's two major linguistic groups in particular, and the city's different ethnocultural communities in general. *Doing the Heart Good* has been criticised for submitting its message too plainly. However, by the end of the novel the reader should have become aware that there is no room for subtlety if one desires to penetrate to the thick-skinned, opinionated Alistair Mackenzie and shake him out of his complacency. Therefore it needs an overtly symbolic incident to bring about the novel's central rapprochement between Mackenzie and Tremblay.

The eventual détente between the opposing neighbours is prompted by no smaller event than the "terror of conflagration" caused by a group of adolescents – and there are explicit indications that they are Anglophones – who put fire on Tremblay's fleur-de-lis flag. To convey the full meaning and dimensions of such an act of wilful vandalism, the incident unfolds on Quebec's national holiday. While June 24 has become an official holiday for all Québécois, the day remains above all a celebration of French Canadian culture and is particularly important to francophone Quebecers. Mackenzie talks of the day as "*their* public holiday, their day for painting themselves blue and white and enshrouding themselves in the flag."[331] Similar to Laurel in Proulx's "Les aurores montréales," Mackenzie deindividuates the Other by referring to Francophones simply in the third person plural. Furthermore, by projecting the identity of the Other onto Franco-Quebecers, Mackenzie establishes a relation to them that could as well have been defined by different criteria, because otherness is not an objective categorisation or inherent quality of anyone but the narrator's way to dissociate himself and to keep *them* at a distance. Tremblay embodies the francophone Other until he and his anglophone neighbour become more frequently and personally involved with each other, so that it gets increasingly difficult not to recognise

---

[329] BISSOONDATH, *DHG*, 135.
[330] BISSOONDATH, *DHG*, 200.
[331] BISSOONDATH, *DHG*, 304 (my italics).

Tremblay as an individual. After Tremblay has saved Mackenzie, including his war medals, the latter experiences a decisive revelation:

> I see that, standing beside me, is Tremblay. His face is drawn; his eyes are wet, his cheeks tear-stained. He says, 'M'sieur Mackenzie, they put...' [...] 'My flag, M'sieur Mackenzie, they put fire to my flag.'
> Dear God...
> The stretcher begins rolling once more, and the body of the ambulance swallows me. I struggle to raise my head. 'Miss-your Tremblay!' I shout. 'Thank you, Miss-your Tremblay!' [...] My hands reach for the medal box, fingers clutching at the wood, and it strikes me as curious that it should be there, safe with me: why should Tremblay have thought of rescuing it? In the confusion of the moment, it occurs to me that I may never see him again. The tragedy of folly will cause us to go our separate ways.
> And to my surprise, the thought does my heart no good, no good at all. The thought of not seeing Tremblay again, I mean.[332]

This urge of explaining himself, of repeating and explicitly expressing his feeling in the last sentence, evidences that Mackenzie has yet to digest this new circumstance that he has to acknowledge to himself a regard for Tremblay. In addition, this excerpt implies that Mackenzie has to admit something else as well, namely that he has misjudged his neighbour in numerous respects. The war medals, for example, are another recurrent symbol in the novel. Mackenzie treasures them as tangible memories of his efforts during WWII and once shows them even to Tremblay, who then asks whether they were worth the trouble. Arrogantly, Mackenzie forbears from going into the matter, imputing a lack of understanding to Tremblay. However, by rescuing the medals from the fire, Tremblay demonstrates that he has been unfairly accused, because he does understand how much these tokens mean to his neighbour. Bissoondath additionally alludes here to the bitter debate about conscription, which was another highly charged issue in English-French relations in Canada at the time of the First and Second World War.

Doing the Heart Good could also be categorised as a sort of *Bildungsroman* in that it traces the evolution of its protagonist, who eventually comes of age, though unusually late in life. By the end of the narrative Mackenzie has gained the wisdom that was so long denied to him. In the paragraph quoted below he takes stock of his life:

> Have I learned anything through this long life of mine? Yes. Unequivocally yes. A certain measure of humility that has been decades coming to me. I was born to a people to whom a sense of entitlement was innate. Even if my family were not among the blessed with mansions and chauffeured cars, there were always others, like Tremblay, who were below us.

---

[332] BISSOONDATH, *DHG*, 324-25.

> Even in our modest circumstances, we came from among the winners. It's not as if we lived every day with this sense, not as if we awoke every morning energized by the knowledge of our supremacy. We were, rather, unconsciously shaped by it. We felt ourselves to be special by virtue of history, by the levers of power some within our community controlled.[333]

Not only does the narrator draw up a balance sheet of his personal history, but also of the history of English-French relations in Quebec. Born in 1920, Alistair Mackenzie grew up in a society in which anglophone superiority was still largely undisputed. Consequently he adopted an outlook on life according to which he felt justified in looking down on Francophones, such as Tremblay. It has taken him decades, he says, to become aware that Quebec society has undergone a profound restructuring, including a more just distribution of power that was once chiefly claimed by members of the anglophone community. The acclaimed Québécois writer and filmmaker Jacques Godbout reflects on these changes in post-1960 Quebec and prognosticates the following in 1989:

> It is its cosmopolitan nature that will ensure Montreal's future. I do not mean by that exotic restaurants, trendy boutiques or cafés; I mean a population that has come from all over the world, that accepts French as a natural fact, English as a convenient means of communication, and that will create a diversified culture grafted on a French-speaking tree.[334]

Though not without struggles, Mackenzie in the end cannot help but be part of such a diversified, predominantly francophone culture and accept his status as a member of a minority now considerably reduced in influence.

The conclusion of the conflicts between the anglophone Mackenzie and the francophone Tremblay indicates that all their contention in the past basically boiled down to the language difference. Some time after the fire forced each of them to go their separate ways, Mackenzie phones his former neighbour:

> A silence falls between us, but unlike the old days, it is not charged. We each, I suspect, have tallied our losses, mourn them, would like to make whole again what we can. Too much has been wasted in mindless bickering. Still, I can think of nothing else to say. 'Well, Tremblay, it was good hearing your voice. I should go now. I just wanted to wish you and your wife –'
> 'You want to hear somet'ing funny, M'sieur Mackenzie?' he says.
> 'Go ahead.'
> 'I am learning Spanish. *Si, sen-your*. Evening course. My wife and me, we plan a big voyage next year. To Espagne.'
> I find myself chuckling. 'Maybe I should take Spanish lessons, too.'
> 'You come with us!' He laughs.
> 'No, no. I was just thinking about you and me, Tremblay. We need a new language, a new way of speaking to each other.'

---

[333] BISSOONDATH, *DHG*, 344-45.
[334] Godbout cited in BISSOONDATH (1994), 192-93.

> He is silent again for a moment. Then he says, 'We have not need of Spanish, M'sieur Mackenzie. You come, make a visit. We will find the new language, you and me.'
> Now it is my turn to fall silent. 'How far is it to your new home, Miss-your Tremblay?'
> 'Not far,' he says.
> I suddenly know that it doesn't matter how far it is, I will find a way to get there.[335]

Despite Mackenzie's eagerness to overcome the disunion with his former antagonist, he does not concede as far as to resorting to the other's language but prefers finding a new one instead, perhaps in order to start afresh on an equal footing. However, Tremblay suggests that their feud has not been a question of English, French or Spanish for that matter but of the personal implications the other's mother tongue once held for them. Hence, if they adapted their mentality, there would be no need to change linguistically, so to speak. Mackenzie's willingness to lay to rest his anti-French principles manifests itself more and more perceptibly. This is how their phone conversation ends:

> 'I must go now. We will talk again?'
> 'Bientôt, M'sieur Mackenzie.'
> One more thing. *Joyeux Noël*, Miss-your Tremblay. And *joyeux Noël* to your wife, too.'
> 'Merry Christmas, Mister Mackenzie. '*asta la vista!*'[336]

It seems to be quite a concession for someone like Alistair Mackenzie to finally express his wishes in Tremblay's language, especially after he has affected not only a deep aversion but also complete ignorance of French until then. Tremblay, for his part, meets him halfway and calls his neighbour "Mister Mackenzie," who has always pretended to be extremely annoyed by being addressed as "*Monsieur.*" In short, their dialogue shows that they are well on their way to find the new language they were talking about. Additionally, some readers may wonder where but in Montreal such a linguistically mixed conversation could authentically take place.

Subsequent to this denouement, Bissoondath includes an addendum, in which he recounts how Mackenzie's dealings with the other characters in the novel are resolved. As far as the anglophone-francophone dichotomy is concerned, it is crucial that the protagonist fully recognises his son-in-law at last, although it costs him some effort to cease to call Jacques "Jack":

> Jack, standing at his place, raises his glass to me. 'Joyeux Noël, m'sieur le professeur.'
> Agnes, sitting in her seat, does the same. 'Merry Christmas, father.'
> 'And to you both.' I acknowledge each with a tip of my glass – 'Agnes' – and with a quick intake of breath: '*Zhack.*' To his pleased smile I add, 'With profound apologies to Miss-your Molière, of course.'[337]

---

[335] BISSOONDATH, *DHG*, 335.
[336] BISSOONDATH, *DHG*, 336.

As in Proulx's narratives, humour is used to remedy tension and palliates Mackenzie's humility in this instance. In conclusion to his epiphantic experiences, the narrator ends his story on an optimistic note and predicts a bright future with regard to anglophone-francophone relations in Montreal. He does so by referring to his relationship with François, implying that there is a way to overcome the language barrier that has previously separated him from his grandson:

> For no reason at all, François sets his eyes on me. He smiles, and it is like the dawn of a thousand suns, shining its light into a future, his and mine, which I know to be there even though I cannot see it.
> He has his mother's eyes. A breathless silence.
> So everything changes, again.[338]

Bissoondath closes the novel with almost the same wording with which he opened it, when Mackenzie begins his narrative after having lost his home to arson. Thus the burning of Tremblay's flag precipitates the major upheavals in Mackenzie's sheltered, carefree existence and his urge to re-evaluate his life. Moreover, the cyclical structure reflects the narrator's need to relive certain events in order to reach his ultimate understanding.

Proulx's short story collection is also cyclical in that it finishes with a narrative that ties up potentially loose ends from the previous ones and broaches issues that recur throughout the entire book. Like the other five 'colour stories,' "*Blanc*" is written in epistolary form, but this time the narrator directly addresses another main character (*"je vous lis ces lignes à voix très basse, en manière de prière pour vous et de berceuse pour moi"*).[339] "*Blanc*" is about a "strange blind date"[340] between the narrator, a young francophone woman who has returned to Montreal after a two-year absence, and the anglophone Mister Murphy, who is on the brink of death. The woman signed up for a benevolent programme and now finds herself assisting Mister Murphy during his last moments. Again and again there is a political subtext in the stories of *Les Aurores montréales*, as is the case in the present one. Yet, although "*Blanc*" lends itself to an analysis of francophone-anglophone interactions in Montreal, it would be reductionist to restrict its interpretation to just this one aspect. There are several other elements at interplay, notably the story's discussion of human relationships, as the protagonist accompanies a young man to his death. Furthermore, Proulx returns to the

---

[337] BISSOONDATH, *DHG*, 344.
[338] BISSOONDATH, *DHG*, 345.
[339] PROULX, *AM*, 239.
[340] PROULX, *AM*, 237.

themes developed in other short stories of the collection, such as loneliness, alienation and the desire to belong. Both characters in "*Blanc*" seem lost. One faces his ultimate exile – death – and shares the last days of his life with a complete stranger, while another, a *Québécoise de souche* feels uprooted in her home town and unsatisfied in various respects, which manifests itself among other things in her sexual fantasies.

Similar to Bissoondath's novel, "*Blanc*" can be described as a coming-of-age story. Yet, the coming of age is not solely of the narrator but also of Montreal. The young Francophone left a Montreal that kept her a child, she says, and comes back after two years to find herself entirely disoriented in the metropolis. Having left immediately after the referendum, she notes a change between pre- and post-referendum Montreal upon her return:

> Montréal n'avait que de vieilles chicanes de clôtures à ressasser, et je détestais cela, Mister Murphy, et j'aimais détester cela et me languir d'autres métropoles plus fertiles en stimuli guerriers. Depuis le référendum, peut-être, où vous-même, alors debout et pétaradant de santé, avez selon toute vraisemblance voté contre l'avènement du fait français en Amérique, depuis l'issue du référendum, peut-être Montréal a-t-il subtilement perdu sa provincialité défensive en même temps que sa cause, et revêtu peu à peu à mon insu la peau coriace des vraies villes, celles où il faut apprendre à devenir quelqu'un tout seul, sans soutien patriotique.[341]

The narrator argues that there is something reassuring yet lacking about Montreal's 'wars,' referring to the age-old language battles fought daily in its streets and to the population's concomitant ethno-linguistic divisions. At the same time the Francophone characterises the anglophone Mister Murphy as the Other, the historical enemy, who in all likelihood "voted against the accession of the French fact in America" in the referendum. However, she suggests that Montreal has in the meantime emancipated itself, lost its "defensive provincialism" and metamorphosed into a true city made up of individuals, who have to identify without recourse to convenient but often loaded categorisation such as 'nationalist' or 'Québécois *de souche*.' Consequently it would not make sense to pigeonhole Mister Murphy as an Anglophone opposed to Francophones. Asserting culture's quintessential hybridity, Edward Said likewise rejects essentialist conceptualisations of identity:

> No one today is purely *one* thing. Labels like Indian, or woman, or Muslim, or American are no more than starting-points, which if followed into actual experience for only a moment are quickly left behind. [...] No one can deny the persisting continuities of long traditions, sustained habitations, national languages, and cultural geographies, but there seems

---

[341] PROULX, *AM*, 232.

no reason except fear and prejudice to keep insisting on their separation and distinctiveness, as if that was all human life was about. Survival in fact is about the connections between things.[342]

In "*Blanc*," the two characters also cease to be strangers as soon as they enter into contact with one another. The narrator admits that the actual reality of their encounter does not correspond to what she expected: "*J'ai honte, Mister Murphy. J'ai honte d'avoir pensé qu'il serait facile d'assister à votre mort comme à un spectacle édifiant, j'ai honte d'avoir cru que vous pourriez demeurer jusqu'à la fin anonyme.*"[343] Instead of an anonymous, old dying man, the woman has to deal with an individual in all his complexities, who, moreover, appears as alive as herself. She realises, in short, that the Other's otherness can be disconcertingly small.

As a result of her encounter with the Other, which takes place at the liminal space[344] between life and death, the narrator experiences an awakening of almost religious dimensions. After a few days as a volunteer in palliative care, she forgets the reasons for her being with Mister Murphy and feels terribly cheated, when he falls into a semicoma on the seventh day. Through this biblical allusion, Proulx constructs a world that does away with categories such as 'anglophone' or 'francophone.' The last sentence of the short story collection thus goes as follows:

> Tout à l'heure, quand vous vous échapperez complètement de votre gangue devenue si encombrante, quand vous ne serez plus ni anglophone ni montréalais ni homme, mais essence volatile affranchie de l'obscurité, je me sentirai un instant moi aussi comme un espace vierge, John, je serai comme vous une page blanche sur laquelle rien n'est encore écrit.[345]

This paragraph is introduced with the image of snow, which, as in the first story of *Les Aurores montréales*, is a symbol of hope and transformation. Snow can cover up hideous or disagreeable things, on a metaphorical level also divisions between people. Feeling like a virgin space herself, the narrator implies that it would be liberating to meet the Other like a *tabula rasa*, unprejudiced and unbiased. Thus, Proulx ends this short story about a Francophone and an Anglophone with the idea of opening a new page – a blank page to write a new history of anglophone-francophone relations in Montreal.

However, Proulx kills off the Anglo after all in the last story of the collection. Could it be an act of catharsis subsequent to the disappointment resulting from the

---

[342] SAID, 336.
[343] PROULX, *AM*, 234.
[344] This evokes again Bhabha's third space "which enables other positions to emerge" and where new forms of identity can come into being (Bhabha qtd. in RUTHERFORD, 211).
[345] PROULX, *AM*, 239.

outcome of the 1995 referendum, shortly after which the book was published? This seems to be very unlikely, especially if one considers that the author promotes exchange and reconciliation between Montreal's different communities throughout her stories. Besides, it is precisely the point of "*Blanc*" that Mister Murphy is not *the* Anglophone in the narrative; he is not supposed to be representative of anybody but to be treated as the individual he is, which ultimately makes it impossible for the protagonist to remain unaffected by his death. If it is desirable to kill anything, then surely one should kill the old stereotypes connected with such labels like 'Anglo.'

This morbid sombreness does not contradict Proulx's characteristic call for humour and a certain lightness. In "*Blanc*," she also lets the narrator exclaim that "*c'est la légèreté qui nous manque le plus dans cette vie de plomb où nous n'apprenons qu'à peupler de nos anxiétés l'univers merveilleux, merveilleusement vide.*"[346] In fact, Proulx advocates cordiality and human warmth at the same time as criticising a lack of humour in a number of her stories. Examples include "*Gris et blanc*," in which a young Hispanophone writes to his friend that laughter is forbidden after a certain hour, or "*Noir et blanc*," whose narrator tells Malcolm X that if he had had a bit of humour, he would still be around, perhaps in Montreal, his feet in the snow instead of underground.[347] In "*Blanc*," Proulx's irony becomes apparent in the narrator's spiritualism. The young woman writes that she can no longer recognise her friends, who have converted to Buddhism after the upsetting events of the referendum. She herself reads the "*Livre tibétain de la vie et de la mort*," where it says that

> il n'y a pas de générosité plus grande que d'accompagner un être humain dans sa mort, au moment précisément où les vivants ne le considèrent plus comme un des leurs et l'abandonnent à son infamie personnelle.[348]

But she concludes by saying to Mister Murphy, "*Mais je ne suis pas généreuse. Si je suis ici, c'est parce que j'ai besoin de vous bien plus que vous avez besoin de moi.*"[349] The two characters in "*Blanc*" depend on each other and it is only through the Other that the narrator finally reconnects with Montreal. Hence, Mister Murphy's death does not result in a sad ending of the narrative but rather a new beginning for the

---

[346] PROULX, *AM*, 238.
[347] "*Le rire, voilà surtout ce qui t'a défaut, mon pauvre vieux Malcolm. Dieu sait où tu serais aujourd'hui si un peu d'humour était venu alléger ton regard sous tes grosses horribles lunettes. À Montréal, peut-être, les deux pieds dans la neige au lieu de les avoir sous terre.*" (PROULX, *AM*, 143).
[348] PROULX, *AM*, 233.
[349] Ibid.

woman. Myriam Amrane writes the following on Montreal's bridging power in Proulx's book:

> Montréal est le symbole du pont qui relie le même et l'autre, la vie et la mort, la tradition et la modernité, elle est le lieu qui réconcilie les contraires et leur permet de cohabiter, le lieu où le narrateur (ou la narratrice) est toujours dans un entre-deux culturel, ethnique, social et à besoin de l'altérité pour se compléter et vivre en harmonie non seulement avec lui-même mais aussi avec son contexte.[350]

The Montreal in *"Blanc"* is such a place where Self and Other meet and merge, even transcending death; a place where seeming opposites can co-exist. After all, survival, as Said suggested, "is about the connections between things."

The deathbed is a peculiar contact zone for a *rendezvous* between the Francophone and the Anglophone. Yet, it is in this contact zone that they develop a new language for each other, similar to Mackenzie and Tremblay in *Doing the Heart Good*. The narrator recalls:

> Vous vous êtes essayé à quelques mots de français, ce dialecte de perdants que vous n'avez jamais voulu maîtriser même en vivant à Montréal, mais cela vous a vite épuisé. Et bientôt, les mots de n'importe quelle langue vous ont paru insuffisants, et vous m'avez montré des photos.[351]

Like Alistair Mackenzie, Mister Murphy appears to be an Anglophone of the old mindset, refusing to learn French, even though he lives in the largest city of an officially francophone society. The encounter with the "french chick"[352] consequently seems to be an epiphantic experience for him as well and so he shares with her most intimate details of his life, before each of them transforms into a "white page on which nothing is yet written."

---

[350] AMRANE, 167.
[351] PROULX, *AM*, 235.
[352] PROULX, *AM*, 234.

5. Outlook and Conclusion

A world in which Alistair Mackenzie finally brings his lips to pronounce a tentative "*Zhack,*" in which Nick Rosenfeld utters a tender "I'm sorry" that Éliane accepts gracefully, and where Laurel is eager to get rid of his *cahier rouge* as well as his ignorance and instead helps his mother serve Anglophones in the store ("Exquiouse me, can I help you?") surely augurs well for the state of francophone-anglophone relations in Montreal. There is no use, however, in painting an over-idealised picture of the situation, because in all likelihood there will always remain a certain degree of tension between the two linguistic communities (and, of course, literature is not a mirror of reality). But this tension can be productive, as evidenced by Montreal's imaginative fertility, and should not obscure the fact that there is also increasing comprehension between Anglophones and Francophones; not just on a purely linguistic level, but also with regard to their different cultural sensibilities.

With the turn of the millennium, Montreal has come to a new self-understanding, redefining itself as a place of diversity. Talking about the spirit of contemporary Montreal, Sherry Simon remarks that it is "a city whose Differences have been downgraded to differences."[353] Similarly, Jocelyn Maclure argues in her analysis (2003) of Quebec's pluralistic society:

> Difference, whether it be sexual, cultural, linguistic, gender-based, or another kind, is starting to be seen as a wellspring from which identity can draw, instead of a problem it has to solve. The expansion and fissuring of the centre is proceeding slowly, it is true, but no more slowly in Quebec than in other nominally liberal societies.[354]

This new valorisation of otherness is expressed in *Les Aurores montréales* as well as in *Doing the Heart Good* – two texts that exteriorise difference and solitude. Their portrayal of how the characters gradually deal with the Other effectively reflects some of the positive changes that have taken place in Montreal in the aftermath of the 1995 sovereignty referendum.

Beyond the realm of literature, there are several other definite signs of a growing rapprochement between Francophones and Anglophones. The *Commission des Etats généreux sur la situation et l'avenir de la langue française au Québec* (Commission of the Estates general on the situation and future of the French language in Quebec), created by the Parti Québécois government of Quebec in 2000, stressed in

---

[353] SIMON (2006), 212. See also page 171.
[354] MACLURE, 137.

its final report that Anglophones were not their enemies but a constituent part of Quebec's reality. "We are turning the page on the 'two solitudes,'"[355] declared one of the two anglophone commissioners. The report affirmed that after twenty-five years of language legislation, French is a language *"pour tout le monde"* and acknowledged as the common language in Quebec by the majority of anglophone groups.[356] Furthermore, the report proclaims that Anglophones are no longer defined as a minority in Quebec but as a *"communauté québécoise de langue anglaise."*[357]

A number of events in 2009 also bespeak a certain equilibrium in French-English relations in Quebec. The *Université de Montréal*, for instance, offered for the first time eight courses in English as part of its summer programme. Jean-François Lisée, the executive director of the university's *Centre d'études et de recherches internationales*, declared, "We're breaking through a wall [...]. It's something that maybe couldn't have happened 15 years ago."[358] A further incident that seemed to have reached a satisfactory conclusion for both linguistic groups was the performance of two Anglo bands, who had at first been banned, at a concert during the Fête Nationale celebrations in Montreal. According to Lisée, the episode was a great day for Quebec nation-building: "Imagine, anglos banging on the doors to get in on the Fête Nationale."[359] A journalist of the anglophone Montreal daily *The Gazette* comments:

> There's general agreement among rational folk that the episode was in the end a reassuring demonstration of how French-English relations have evolved to a level of relatively comfortable accommodation that sits well with a majority of both language communities. It would be an exaggeration to say that language peace reigns unperturbed in the land of Quebec, but the last major English-French confrontations – over bilingual signs – was 20 years ago and while there have been occasional eruptions of hostility since, they have tended to be over lesser grievances that were soon passed over.[360]

Another reporter of the same newspaper tried to answer the question why young Anglophones are not leaving Quebec as they did a generation ago. He suggests that it is not only because they speak better French and are not "being chased away by politi-

---

[355] Qtd. in Josée BOILEAU. "Larose prêche la réconciliation." *Le Devoir* 21 Aug. 2001. See also OAKES and WARREN, 151.
[356] Cf. Gérald Larose qtd. in BOILEAU.
[357] Ibid.
[358] Qtd. in Hubert BAUCH. "Breaking Through Quebec's Language Barrier." *Montreal Gazette* 20 June 2009.
[359] Ibid.
[360] BAUCH (20 June 2009).

cal uncertainty," but also because, by the 1990s, a "cultural shift" had made speaking English "more acceptable in Quebec."[361]

This more harmonious modus vivendi between Francophones and Anglophones in post-1995 Quebec is also due to the fact that Anglo-Quebecers have more or less accepted their minority status.[362] Dickinson and Young (2008) argue that "[y]oung anglophones in particular, themselves products of the language provisions under Bill 101, seem quite comfortable as a minority in an increasingly pluralist Montreal."[363] In a study published in 2006 it was found that over forty per cent of the young Anglophones surveyed "considered themselves as much members of the Francophone community as the Anglophone community."[364] This attitude evidences a sense of identification with bi- or multilingualism – probably with heterogeneity and diversity in general – in Montreal.

For these young Quebecers, the acrimonious disputes of pre-1995 Quebec might elude their comprehension today. Richler's non-fiction essay *Oh Canada! Oh Quebec!*,[365] for instance, including the torrent of heated and passionate debates it unleashed, may appear to some a mere curiosity of the past. It remains questionable whether Richler's "nightmare" was justified:

> A Quebecer born and bred, I suffer from a recurring nightmare that all of us, French- and English-speaking, will one day be confronted by our grandchildren, wanting to know what our generation was about then the Berlin Wall crumbled, a playwright became president of Czechoslovakia, and, after seventy-four years, the Communist Party way overthrown in the Soviet Union and then the Soviet Union itself was dissolved. We will be honor bound to reply, why, in Quebec, we were hammering each other over whether or not bilingual commercial signs could be posted outside as well as inside. We were in heat, not only in this

---

[361] David JOHNSTON. "'Cultural Shift' Made English More Acceptable." *Montreal Gazette* 29 Jan. 2009. One has to emphasise, however, that this opinion is pronounced by Montreal's major anglophone newspaper.

[362] Oakes and Warren write that an "Anglophone or English Quebec identity only really came into being during the late 1960s and 1970s, the period during which *Québécois* came to replace 'French Canadian' to describe the collective identity of the Francophone majority" and that "Quebec's Anglophones were unaware of their minority status before the rise of a Quebec identity" (OAKES and WARREN, 152). Yet, within the province they had been numerically in the minority before that, but they had formed an elite. Therefore, it would be more accurate to state that Anglophones have now largely reconciled themselves to the fact that they are no longer a *privileged* minority.

[363] DICKINSON and YOUNG, 361.

[364] Qtd. in OAKES and WARREN, 170.

[365] McGimpsey describes Richler's satire as Montreal's "cursed potboiler: a book actually read and debated by people who did not go to college, a book frequently discussed by those who never read it." (MCGIMPSEY, 163).

province, but throughout Canada, over whether or not Quebec could be officially crowned "a distinct society."[366]

However, language and its implications will most likely continue to be a highly emotional issue;[367] in fact, the ongoing debate seems to have become part of Québécois culture.

Yet, there are critical voices as well, who question whether Francophones and Anglophones are in the process of reconciliation. Genetsch, for example, maintains that "the gulf between the two so-called founding nations appears to be widening, and isolation rather than MacLennan's (i.e. Rilke's) caressing solitudes characterises the relationship between English and Franco-Canada."[368] This was perhaps the case at the time of the referenda,[369] but within the province the current trend is generally towards a more inclusive society. The political scientist Alain Gagnon said after an absence of a few years:

> When I came back to Quebec I found a new society in Quebec. I'm very impressed by the rapprochement between the two communities. There's more and more complicity, in the workplace, in festivals, in local political organizations where before anglophones were in their milieu and francophones in theirs. That's a very positive change and it confirms that Quebec is becoming a globally inclusive society, and that's good for everyone.[370]

Still, not everybody would agree with that statement. André Pratte, writing for *La Presse*, concedes that relations between the country's two principal linguistic groups have been fairly harmonious in recent years, but only because Anglophones have avoided confrontations. He moreover claims that there is still a lot of incomprehension between the two communities and that *"les francophones ont du mal à voir les anglo-Québécois autrement que comme une minorité dominante et menaçante."*[371] A

---

[366] Mordecai RICHLER. *Oh Canada! Oh Quebec!: Requiem for a Divided Country*. Toronto: Penguin Books, 1992. 236.

[367] A recent example of an emotional sociolinguistic commentary includes a book called *La Grande Langue: Éloge de l'Anglais* by André Brochu, a retired literature professor, writer and current member of the *Académie des lettres du Québec*. What the author entitled *essai-fiction* is a satirical, yet bitter invective against the English language. At times self-deprecating, at others vitriolic, Brochu writes: *"La Grande Langue affirmait chaque jour davantage sa suprématie et, même chassée des vitrines de Montréal et du reste du Québec, elle occupait désormais dans les cœurs la place laissée vacante par la religion [...]. Pourquoi pas l'anglais ? C'est une langue sportive, universelle. Elle est la meilleure garantie contre le narcissisme national. Il faut en finir avec l'identité. Il faut être autre, parler autre [...]. Je parle anglais ! je parle anglais ! et toutes mes fautes me sont remises."* (André BROCHU. *La Grande Langue: Éloge de l'Anglais*. Montréal: XYZ Editeur, 2002. 28, 11, 24).

[368] GENETSCH, 3.

[369] Cf. KOLBOOM and LETOURNEAU, 39.

[370] Qtd. in BAUCH (20 June 2009).

[371] André PRATTE. "Un nouveau dialogue." *La Presse* 29 March 2005.

2005 poll commissioned by *La Presse* might give a similar impression of the situation in Quebec. Quebecers were surveyed on their attitudes towards voting for a woman, a Black, a homosexual and an Anglophone as premier of Quebec, with the result that the strongest opposition (35%) was towards an anglophone premier. However, one has to interpret such surveys critically; that is to say that the poll did not necessarily represent the actual opinions about Anglophones. Yet, the results did reveal that speaking ill of Anglophones is acceptable and accepted, that anglophobia can be more openly expressed than xenophobia or misogyny, because Anglo-Québécois are not protected to the same extent by political correctness.[372]

In addition, public discourse continues to exploit military vocabulary to refer to the language situation in Quebec. One reads regularly about the "threat" or "invasion" of English in francophone newspapers.[373] Apart from that, the notion of the two solitudes is still widely used, as in "Two Solitudes on Prevalence of French in Montreal: Poll." In this article, it states that nearly ninety per cent of Francophones agreed with the view that French is threatened in Montreal, while fewer than a quarter of non-Francophones did so.[374] The survey thus shows that the survival of French in Montreal remains a perennial concern and cause for a high level of insecurity among the city's francophone population. On a more alarmist note, Poisson exclaims that Montreal is becoming anglophone and articulates his regret that Francophones too often think that the "battle" is already lost:

> La tension monte entre francophones d'un côté et anglophones et allophones de l'autre. Malheureusement, nous continuons trop souvent, en tant que francophones, à croire que ça ne vaut pas la peine, que le combat est terminé et que, de toute façon, c'est déjà perdu. [...] Une chose est certaine, c'est aux francophones que revient le choix de garder ou de céder leur place. Ils auront plus de chance en cessant d'accuser « l'autre » et en affirmant haut et fort leur identité culturelle.[375]

A similar debate is going on about French-English bilingualism and whether it is to the detriment of French. Assuming that language is not a religion, where one is either Muslim or Catholic, Marco Micone concludes:

> Le français n'est pas en péril. La complexité de la situation de la région de Montréal exige des analystes qu'ils tiennent compte de multiples critères, désethnicisent enfin la notion de francophone et se souviennent que nous sommes encore dans une phase de transition.[376]

---

[372] Cf. Yves BOISVERT. "On va les avoir, les Anglais." *La Presse* 30 June 2005. See also André PRATTE. "Notre maître, le passé." *La Presse* 4 July 2005. OAKES and WARREN, 158-61.
[373] Cf. RICHER, for instance.
[374] Cf. M. SCOTT.
[375] POISSON.
[376] MICONE.

In 2002, a journalistic experiment that involved the swapping of newspapers, press offices and languages also scrutinised the topic of bilingualism in Montreal. While the anglophone *Gazette* opted for the headline "Bilingualism? Pas de problème," *La Presse* did not downplay the potentially problematic nature of bilingualism and shifted the question mark to the end of the phrase: "Bilingualisme, No Problem?"[377] Moreover, the francophone journalist Matthieu Perreault writes that "both the Francophone and the Anglophone communities are slowly learning to disentangle language and emotion. For Anglophones, it seems an easier task."[378]

Different people and members of different language groups will proffer different accounts of the sociolinguistic and cultural situation in Montreal, which continues to be ambiguous. One thing seems safe to say, namely that everybody, in fact, belongs to a minority – Anglophones on a provincial and Francophones on a national level and in the North American context. Of course, the anglophone community is, in its very constitution, a priori "unable to transcend linguistic boundaries in order to integrate completely"[379] into Quebec society. But, as Sherry Simon proposes, in a "postcolonial Montreal characterized by cultural plurality and relations of diversity" there is the "possibility of the co-existence of many vocabularies within a single national grammar."[380]

The notorious 'two solitudes' may not yet have reached the stage of having metamorphosed into 'two solicitudes,' as suggested by the book of the same title by Margaret Atwood and Victor-Lévy Beaulieu. However, notwithstanding their differences, there is increasing exchange and mixing between the two linguistic communities.[381] Numerous factors[382] have contributed to the amelioration of anglophone-francophone relations in the late twentieth and twenty-first century in Montreal. To-

---

[377] Cf. OAKES and WARREN, 166. The authors remark that "the very fact that both newspapers agreed to the swap tells us something about the state of relations between the two communities."

[378] Qtd. in OAKES and WARREN, 167.

[379] OAKES and WARREN, 151-52.

[380] SIMON (2006), 172.

[381] This mixing is not just restricted to language, but it can also take the form of exogamy, that is, marriages between Anglophones and Francophones (or Allophones), whose children are then "bilingual and profoundly bicultural"(Jedwab qtd. in OAKES and WARREN, 169). In 2001, the proportion of exogamous couples was 55%, 44% of which were anglophone/francophone couples (ibid).

[382] Although several of the most pertinent ones have been addressed, this study makes no claim to exhaustivity. Some aspects are omitted, such as the economic recovery in Canada beginning in the mid-1990s. (Suffice to say – in the scope of the present study – that given the economic and political climate during the 1980s and early 1990s, the overall level of dissatisfaction was very high and exacerbated French-English relations; the impact of the subsequent economic recovery has been particularly pronounced in Quebec).

day, Franco-Quebecers are much more confident than they were prior to the early 1990s and the French language has become a container and expression of a variety of histories and identities. Furthermore, Montrealers exhibit a disposition to deal actively with the Other to make the pluricentric city a liveable place for everybody. After all, whatever their cultural and linguistic differences are, Montreal's citizens are bound together by sharing the same geo-political space; their joint experience of the metropolis affords them a common language.

Though not always or necessarily congruent with cultural and socioeconomic actualities, literature reflects, in part, Montreal's reality. Sherry Simon emphasises, "It is contact and interaction (not isolation and exclusion) that fuel the work of many Montreal writers – in English and French"; and she concludes, "Being alive to difference is a permanent obligation."[383] In a 2002 interview, Monique Proulx forwards a similar view, while explaining her adoration of Montreal:

> Je la [i.e. the city of Montreal] vois de plus en plus comme une ville pleine de richesses ; pas dans le sens de la gentrification, bien sûr, mais dans celui d'une maturité : je trouve que les Montréalais vivent de plus en plus dans le respect les uns des autres. Le fait que l'on puisse voir dans une même rue des francophones, des Grecs, ou d'autres, et que le tout ne s'homogénéise pas mais reste en harmonie est réjouissant. C'est une ville qui vibre, qui n'est pas superficielle ; de plus, elle regorge de créateurs, ce qui me plaît énormément.[384]

Today, exactly 250 years after French Canadians were defeated in the Battle of the Plains of Abraham, Francophones and Anglophones – by tacit agreement – choose to get along with each other, as do the characters in the texts analysed in this study. Bissoondath summarises the present situation between the two linguistic communities as follows:

> [D]espite the differences between languages [...] we have acquired an uneasy similarity. Though sometimes blinded by the immediacy of political concerns, we are as a people fundamentally blended: our interest in each other cannot easily be extinguished. The right arm may not resemble the left arm, but they belong together on the same body, serving its interests and their own. Each would be poorer without the other.[385]

It is thus to be hoped that Montreal appreciates its 'ambidexterity' and takes pride in being a multilingual, pluriethnic city, open to difference and diversity.

---

[383] SIMON (2006), 161.
[384] Qtd. in Pascale NAVARRO. "Monique Proulx: Vivre sa vie." *Voir.ca*. 18 April 2002. Communications Voir Inc. 4 Sept. 2009 <http://www.voir.ca/publishing/article.aspx?article=20720&section=10>.
[385] BISSOONDATH (1994), 194.

Bibliography

Primary Sources:

Bissoondath, Neil. *Doing the Heart Good*. London: Scribner, 2002.

-----. "On the Eve of Uncertain Tomorrows." In *Multiculturalism and Immigration in Canada: An Introductory Reader*. Ed. Elspeth Cameron. Toronto: Canadian Scholars' Press, 2004. 327-44.

Dickens, Charles. *A Tale of Two Cities*. 1859. Oxford: Oxford UP, 1988.

MacLennan, Hugh. *Two Solitudes*. 1945. Toronto: General Paperbacks, 1991.

Proulx, Monique. *Homme invisible à la fenêtre*. Québec: Boréal/Seuil, 1993.

-----. *Les Aurores montréales*. 2e éd. Montréal: Boréal compact, 1997.

-----. *Le cœur est un muscle involontaire*. Montréal: Boréal, 2002.

Robin, Régine. *La québécoite*. Montréal: Editions Québec, 1983.

Villeneuve, Gisèle. *Visiting Elizabeth*. Montreal: XYZ Publishing, 2004.

Secondary Sources:

Al-Ali, Nadje and Khalid Koser. "Transnationalism, International Migration and Home." In *New Approaches to Migration? Transnational Communities and the Transformation of Home*. Eds. Nadje Al-Ali and Khalid Koser. London: Routledge, 2002. 1-14.

Amrane, Myriam. "*Les aurores Montréales* de Monique Proulx ou l'appropriation d'un lieu de vie." *Synergies Algérie* 4 (2009): 149-71.

Association des Familles Tremblay. 2009. Le Centre de généalogie francophone d'Amérique. 20 Oct. 2009 <http://www.genealogie.org/famille/tremblay/>.

Atwood, Margaret and Victor-Lévy Beaulieu. *Two Solicitudes: Conversations*. Toronto: McClelland & Stewart, 1998.

Barfoot, Joan. "*Doing the Heart Good* by Neil Bissoondath." *Quill & Quire*. March 2002. St. Joseph Media Inc. 4 Sept. 2009 <http://www.quillandquire.com/reviews/review.cfm?review_id=2631>.

Bauch, Hubert. "Breaking Through Quebec's Language Barrier." *Montreal Gazette* 20 June 2009.

-----. "French-English Relations in Quebec at a 'Happy Medium.'" *Montreal Gazette* 21 June 2009.

Behiels, M.D. "Francophone-Anglophone Relations." *The Canadian Encyclopedia*. 2009. Historica Foundation of Canada. 17 Aug. 2009 <http://www.thecanadianencyclopedia.com/index.cfm?PgNm=TCE&Params=A1SEC820892>.

Beneventi, Domenic. "Lost in the City: The Montreal Novels of Régine Robin and Robert Majzels." In *Downtown Canada: Writing Canadian Cities*. Eds. Justin D. Edwards and Douglas Ivison. Toronto: U of Toronto P, 2005. 104-21.

Bernard, André. "Les répercussions sociales et politiques de la Loi 101." In *Le Français au Québec: 400 ans d'histoire et de vie*. Ed. Michel Plourde. Québec: Fides, 2003. 292-300.

Bhabha, Homi K. "Cultural Diversity and Cultural Differences." In *The Post-Colonial Studies Reader*. Eds. Bill Ashcroft, Gareth Griffiths and Helen Tiffin. London: Routledge, 1995. 206-09.

-----. *The Location of Culture*. London: Routledge, 1994.

Bissoondath, Neil. *Selling Illusions: The Cult of Multiculturalism in Canada*. Toronto: Penguin Books, 1994.

Bliss, J.M. Ed. *Canadian History in Documents: 1763-1966*. Toronto: Ryerson Press, 1966.

Blue, Rick. "No Shortage of Jokes About Anglos." *Montreal Gazette* 26 March 2009.

Blum, Jérôme. "Coat of arms of the province of Quebec." 29 July 2006. *Wikimedia Commons*. 4 Feb. 2011 <http://en.wikipedia.org/wiki/File:Coat_of_arms_of_Qu%C3%A9bec.svg>.

Boileau, Josée. "Larose prêche la réconciliation." *Le Devoir* 21 Aug. 2001.

Boisvert, Yves. "On va les avoir, les Anglais!" *La Presse* 30 June 2005.

Brochu, André. *La Grande Langue: Éloge de l'Anglais*. Montréal: XYZ Editeur, 2002.

Busby, Brian John. "Bissoondath, Neil Devindra." *The Canadian Encyclopedia*. 2009. Historica Foundation of Canada. 4 Sept. 2009 <http://www.thecanadianencyclopedia.com/index.cfm?PgNm=TCE&Params=A1ARTA0010093>.

Butler, Judith. *Gender Trouble: Feminism and the Subversion of Identity*. New York: Routledge, 1990.

Chambers, Iain. "Citizenship, Language, and Modernity." *PMLA* 117.1 (January 2002): 24-31.

-----. *Migrancy, Culture, Identity*. London and New York: Routledge, 1994.

Coleman, Daniel. "Bissoondath, Neil." In *Encyclopedia of Literature in Canada*. Ed. W.H. New. Toronto: U of Toronto P, 2002. 122.

Conlogue, Ray. *Impossible Nation: The Longing for Homeland in Canada and Quebec*. Stratford: The Mercury Press, 1996.

Cook, Margaret. "Proulx, Monique." In *Encyclopedia of Literature in Canada*. Ed. W.H. New. Toronto: U of Toronto P, 2002. 903.

De Certeau, Michel. "Walking in the City." In *The Cultural Studies Reader*. Ed. Simon During. London: Routledge, 1994. 151-60.

Demmerling, Christoph. "Hermeneutik der Alltäglichkeit und In-der-Welt-sein (§§ 25-38)." In *Martin Heidegger, Sein und Zeit*. Ed. Thomas Rentsch. Berlin: Akademie Verlag, 2001. 89-116.

Desmeules, Christian. "Entretien – La vraie nature de Monique Proulx." *Le Devoir* 15/16 March 2008.

Dickinson, John A. "L'anglicisation." In *Le Français au Québec: 400 ans d'histoire et de vie*. Ed. Michel Plourde. Québec: Fides, 2003. 80-92.

Dickinson, John and Brian Young. *A Short History of Quebec*. 4th ed. Montreal: McGill-Queen's UP, 2008.

Dinka, Nicholas. "Hard Questions: Neil Bissoondath Takes on a Controversial Subject in His Timely New Novel." *Quill & Quire*. Sept. 2005. St. Joseph Media Inc. 4 Sept. 2009 <http://www.quillandquire.com/authors/profile.cfm?article_id=6856>.

Dorais, Louis-Jacques. "Immigration, multiculturalisme et identités canadiennes." In *Perspectives de l'Interculturel*. Ed. Jeannine Blomart and Bernd Krewer. Paris: L'Harmattan, 1994. 145-50.

Dufour, Christian and Christine Fréchette. "Bilinguisme > nécessité ou péril?" *La Presse* 2 April 2009.

Dufresne, Jacques. "Le Québec, cobaye et définisseur de la mondialisation." *Grenzgänge* 3 (1995): 9-22.

Dupuis, Gilles. "Transculturalism and *écritures migrantes*." In *History of Literature in Canada: English-Canadian and French-Canadian*. Ed. Reingard M. Nischik. Rochester: Camden House, 2008. 497-508.

Dupuis, Gilles and Klaus-Dieter Ertler. "Introduction." In *A la carte: Le roman québécois (2000-2005)*. Eds. Gilles Dupuis and Klaus-Dieter Ertler. Frankfurt, Wien: Lang, 2007. 9-17.

Eakin, Paul John. *How Our Lives Become Stories: Making Selves*. Ithaca: Cornell UP, 1999.

Edwards, Justin D. and Douglas Ivison. "Epilogue." In *Downtown Canada: Writing Canadian Cities*. Eds. Justin D. Edwards and Douglas Ivison. Toronto: U of Toronto P, 2005. 197-208.

Eibl, Doris. *Romaneske Un-Heimlichkeiten im Spannungsfeld von Postmoderne und "Ecriture au féminin."* Dissertation, University of Innsbruck, 1999.

-----. "The French-Canadian Short Prose Narrative." In *History of Literature in Canada: English-Canadian and French-Canadian*. Ed. Reingard M. Nischik. Rochester: Camden House, 2008. 450-55.

-----. "The French-Canadian Short Story." In *History of Literature in Canada: English-Canadian and French-Canadian*. Ed. Reingard M. Nischik. Rochester: Camden House, 2008. 264-69.

Everett-Heath, John. "Mackenzie." *Concise Dictionary of World Place-Names*. Oxford UP. 2005. *Encyclopedia.com*. 20 Oct. 2009 <http://www.encyclopedia.com/doc/1O209-Mackenzie.html>.

Fanon, Frantz. *Black Skin, White Masks*. 1952. NY: Grove Press, 1967.

Fish, Stanley. "Boutique Multiculturalism, or Why Liberals Are Incapable of Thinking About Hate Speech." *Critical Inquiry* 23.2 (1997): 378-95.

Fisher, Dominique D.. "Transculturalité et délocalisation dans *Les aurores montréales* de Monique Proulx." In *Le Québec à l'aube du nouveau millénaire: Entre tradition et modernité*. Ed. Marie-Christine Weidmann Koop. Québec: Presses de l'Université du Québec, 2008. 308-16.

Freeman, Mark. *Rewriting the Self: History, Memory, Narrative*. London: Routledge, 1993.

Garvie, Maureen. "*Aurora Montrealis* by Monique Proulx." *Quill & Quire*. Dec. 1997. St. Joseph Media Inc. 4 Sept. 2009 <http://www.quillandquire.com/reviews/review.cfm?review_id=270>.

Gauthier, Louise. *La mémoire sans frontières: Emile Ollivier, Naïm Kattan et les écrivains migrants au Québec*. Sainte-Foy: Editions de l'IQRC, 1997.

Genetsch, Martin. *The Texture of Identity: The Fiction of MG Vassanji, Neil Bissoondath and Rohinton Mistry*. Toronto: Tsar Publications, 2007.

George, Rosemary M. *The Politics of Home: Postcolonial Relocations and Twenty-First Century Fiction*. Cambridge: Cambridge UP, 1996.

Gibson, John. *Fiction and the Weave of Life*. Oxford: Oxford UP, 2007.

Glissant, Edouard. *Introduction à une poétique du divers*. Paris: Gallimard, 1996.

Government of Canada. "Elements of the Flag." 17 Nov. 2008. *Canadian Heritage*. 28 Sept. 2009 <http://www.pch.gc.ca/pgm/ceem-cced/symbl/df6-eng.cfm>.

Government of Quebec. "The Charter of the French Language – Preamble." 2002. *Office québécois de la langue française*. 21 Aug. 2009 <http://www.olf.gouv.qc.ca/english/charter/preamble.html>.

Grabbe, Hans-Jürgen and Sabine Schindler. "Introduction." In *The Merits of Memory: Concepts, Contexts, Debates*. Eds. Hans-Jürgen Grabbe and Sabine Schindler. Heidelberg: Winter, 2008. 1-13.

Grutman, Rainier. *Des langues qui résonnent: L'hétérolinguisme au XIXe siècle québécois*. Saint-Laurent: Fides, 1997.

Hall, Stuart. "Cultural Identity and Diaspora." In *Colonial Discourse and Postcolonial Theory: A Reader*. Ed. Patrick Williams and Laura Chrisman. NY: Columbia UP, 1994. 392-403.

-----. "Introduction: Who Needs 'Identity'?" In *Questions of Cultural Identity*. Eds. Stuart Hall and Paul du Gay. London: Sage, 1996. 1-17.

Hammill, Faye. *Canadian Literature*. Edinburgh: Edinburgh UP, 2007.

Holman, Andrew and Robert Thacker. "Literary and Popular Culture." In *Canadian Studies in the New Millennium*. Eds. Patrick James and Mark Kasoff. Toronto: U of Toronto P, 2008. 125-64.

Howells, Coral Ann. Ed. *Where are the Voices Coming From? Canadian Culture and the Legacies of History*. Amsterdam, NY: Rodopi, 2004.

Hutton, Patrick H. "Memory and the Problem of Historical Identity in Our Times." In *The Merits of Memory: Concepts, Contexts, Debates*. Eds. Hans-Jürgen Grabbe and Sabine Schindler. Heidelberg: Winter, 2008. 81-96.

James, Patrick and Mark Kasoff. "Future Prospects." In *Canadian Studies in the New Millennium*. Eds. Patrick James and Mark Kasoff. Toronto: U of Toronto P, 2008. 277-80.

Johnston, David. "'Cultural Shift' Made English More Acceptable." *Montreal Gazette* 29 Jan. 2009.

Kamala, N. "Traduire la diversité: un roman montréalais en anglais." *Synergies Inde* 3 (2008): 69-79.

Karlsen, Kathleen. "Flower Symbolism Guide." *Living Arts Originals*. 13 Sept. 2009. Living Arts Enterprises LLC. 28 Sept. 2009 <http://www.livingartsoriginals.com/infoflowersymbolism.htm>.

Keahey, Deborah. *Making It Home: Place in Canadian Prairie Literature*. Winnipeg: U of Manitoba P, 1998.

King, Nicola. *Memory, Narrative, Identity: Remembering the Self*. Edinburgh: Edinburgh UP, 2000.

Klaus, Peter. "Frankophone und Allophone in Québec: *même combat*? Sprache und Literatur als komplementäre Identitätsparadigmata." *Grenzgänge* 3 (1995): 121-34.

-----. "Introduction." *Neue Romania* 18 (1997): 5-6.

Klinkert, Thomas. *Einführung in die französische Literaturwissenschaft*. Berlin: Schmidt, 2004.

Kolboom, Ingo and Paul Létourneau. "Québec zwischen Integration und Souveränität: Ein kanadisches Dilemma." *Grenzgänge* 3 (1995): 23-41.

Kostash, Myrna. "Imagination, Representation, and Culture." In *Literary Pluralities*. Ed. Christl Verduyn. Peterborough: Broadview Press, 1998. 92-96.

Kristeva, Julia. *Etrangers à nous-mêmes*. Paris: Gallimard, 1988.

Kröller, Eva-Marie. "Introduction." In *The Cambridge Companion to Canadian Literature*. Ed. Eva-Marie Kröller. Cambridge: Cambridge UP, 2004. 1-21.

Kruk, Laurie. "'All Voices Belong to Me' – An Interview with Neil Bissoondath." *Canadian Literature* 180 (Spring 2004): 53-69.

Lakoff, George. *Don't Think of an Elephant! Know Your Values and Frame the Debate*. White River Junction: Chelsea Green Publishing, 2004.

Lamore, Jean. "Transculturation: naissance d'un mot." *Vice Versa* 21 (1987): 18-19.

Leclerc, Catherine and Sherry Simon. "Zones de contact: nouveaux regards sur la littérature anglo-québécoise." *Voix et images* 30.3 (2005): 15-29.

Leitch, Vincent B. et al. Eds. *The Norton Anthology of Theory and Criticism*. New York: W.W. Norton, 2001.

Létourneau, Jocelyn. *A History for the Future: Rewriting Memory and Identity in Quebec*. Montreal: McGill-Queen's UP, 2004.

Linteau, Paul-André. *Histoire de Montréal depuis la Confédération*. 2nd ed. Montréal: Boréal, 2000.

Ltaif, Nadine. "Ecrire pour vivre l'échange entre les langues." In *Literary Pluralities*. Ed. Christl Verduyn. Peterborough: Broadview Press, 1998. 81-83.

Maclure, Jocelyn. *Quebec Identity: The Challenge of Pluralism*. Montreal: McGill-Queen's UP, 2003.

"Malgré nous, nous transportons le Québec sur nos épaules." *Synopsis*. 2000. 2 Sept. 2009 <http://declic.com/synopsis/ monique.htm>.

Mathieu, Jacques. "La naissance d'un nouveau monde." In *Le Français au Québec: 400 ans d'histoire et de vie*. Ed. Michel Plourde. Québec: Fides, 2003. 5-13.

-----. "New France." *The Canadian Encyclopedia*. 2009. Historica Foundation of Canada. 17 Aug. 2009 <http://www.thecanadianencyclopedia.com/index.cfm?PgNm=TCE&Params=A1ARTA0005701>.

Mathis, Ursula. "La poésie québécoise: un bilan." In *Etudes québécoises: bilan et perspectives*. Ed. Hans-Josef Niederehe. Tübingen: Niemeyer, 1996. 131-51.

-----. "'Speak What'?: Observations à propos de la littérature immigrée au Québec." *Neue Romania* 18 (1997): 25-39.

Maury, Nicole and Jules Tessier. *A l'écoute des francophones d'Amérique*. Montréal: Centre éducatif et culturel, 1991.

McGimpsey, David. "A Walk in Montreal: Wayward Steps Through the Literary Politics of Contemporary English Quebec." *Essays on Canadian Writing* 71 (Fall 2000): 150-69.

Michaud, Ginette. "De la 'Primitive Ville' à la Place Ville-Marie: lectures de quelques récits de fondation de Montréal." In *Montréal imaginaire: ville et littérature*. Eds. Gilles Marcotte and Pierre Nepveu. Montréal: Fides, 1992. 13-95.

Micone, Marco. "Le français n'est pas en péril." *Le Devoir* 16 Oct. 1999. 19 Aug. 2009 <http://wwwens.uqac.ca/~flabelle/socio/micone.htm>.

Miller, Katherine. "Rewriting Identity." *Canadian Literature* 177 (Summer 2003): 166-68.

Ministère de la Justice. "Devise et armoiries du Québec." 2009. *Gouvernement du Québec*. 28 Sept. 2009 <http://www.formulaire.gouv.qc.ca/cgi/affiche_doc.cgi?dossier=655&table=0&>.

Montréal, ville francophone. Dir. Jean-Jacques Sheitoyan. Société Radio-Canada, 1992.

Navarro, Pascale. "Monique Proulx: Vivre sa vie." *Voir.ca*. 18 April 2002. Communications Voir Inc. 4 Sept. 2009 <http://www.voir.ca/publishing/article.aspx?article=20720&section=10>.

Neilson Bonikowsky, Laura. "Alexander Mackenzie, Explorer." *The Canadian Encyclopedia*. 2009. Historica Foundation of Canada. 20 Oct. 2009 <http://www.thecanadianencyclopedia.com/index.cfm?PgNm=ArchivedFeatures&Params=A261>.

New, W.H. *A History of Canadian Literature*. Montreal: McGill-Queen's UP, 2001.

Nischik, Reingard M. "The Canadian Short Story: Status, Criticism, Historical Survey." In *The Canadian Short Story: Interpretations*. Ed. Reingard M. Nischik. Rochester: Camden House, 2007. 1-40.

-----. "The English-Canadian Short Story since 1967: Between (Post)Modernism and (Neo)Realism." In *History of Literature in Canada: English-Canadian and French-Canadian*. Ed. Reingard M. Nischik. Rochester: Camden House, 2008. 330-51.

-----. "The Modernist English-Canadian Short Story." In *History of Literature in Canada: English-Canadian and French-Canadian*. Ed. Reingard M. Nischik. Rochester: Camden House, 2008. 194-206.

Oakes, Leigh and Jane Warren. *Language, Citizenship and Identity in Quebec*. Basingstoke: Palgrave Macmillan, 2007.

Office of the Prime Minister. "Prime Minister Addresses Francophonie Summit." 2006. 17 Aug. 2009 <http://pm.gc.ca/eng/media.asp?category=2&id=1338>.

Ortiz, Fernando. *Contrapunteo cubano del tabaco y del azúcar*. 1940. Caracas: Biblioteca Ayacucho, 1987.

Parker, Simon. *Urban Theory and the Urban Experience: Encountering the City*. London: Routledge, 2004.

"Parti Québécois seeks to affirm supremacy of French." *The Gazette* 8 June 2009.

Poisson, Patrick. "Les francophones laissent Montréal s'angliciser." *La Presse* 26 Oct. 2009.

Pöll, Bernhard. *Francophonies périphériques: Histoire, statut et profil des principales variétés du français hors de France*. Paris: L'Harmattan, 2001.

Pratt, Mary Louise. "Arts of the Contact Zone." In *Academic Discourse: Readings for Argument and Analysis*. Ed. Gail Stygall. 3rd ed. Mason, Ohio: Thomson Custom Publishing, 2002. 613-28.

Pratte, André. "Notre maître, le passé." *La Presse* 4 July 2005.

-----. "Un nouveau dialogue." *La Presse* 29 March 2005.

Provencher, Jean. *Chronologie du Québec 1534-2000*. Montréal: Boréal, 2000.

Radford, Jonathan. "The Dahlia in Italy." *Life in Italy*. 28 Sept. 2009 <http://www.lifeinitaly.com/garden/dahlia-italy.asp>.

Richer, Jocelyne. "Luc Plamondon reproche aux politiciens de ne pas défendre la langue française." *Le Soleil* 7 May 2009.

Richler, Mordecai. *Oh Canada! Oh Quebec!: Requiem for a Divided Country*. Toronto: Penguin Books, 1992.

Rocher, Guy. "La politique et la loi linguistiques du Québec en 1977." In *Le Français au Québec: 400 ans d'histoire et de vie*. Ed. Michel Plourde. Québec: Fides, 2003. 273-84.

Rödder, Kristina. "Remembering the 'Good War': World War II, Historiography, and 'Memoriography' at the End of the 20th Century." In *The Merits of Memory: Concepts, Contexts, Debates*. Eds. Hans-Jürgen Grabbe and Sabine Schindler. Heidelberg: Winter, 2008. 263-74.

Russell, Victor L. "Mackenzie, William Lyon." *The Canadian Encyclopedia*. 2009. Historica Foundation of Canada. 20 Oct. 2009 <http://www.thecanadianencyclopedia.com/index.cfm?PgNm=TCE&Params=A1ARTA0004947>.

Rutherford, Jonathan. Ed. "The Third Space: Interview with Homi Bhabha." In *Identity: Community, Culture, Difference*. London: Lawrence & Wishart, 1990. 207-21.

Said, Edward. *Culture and Imperialism*. NY: Knopf, 1993.

Sankar, Celia. "Author of His Own Destiny." *Américas* 53 (July 2001): 46-51.

Saywell, John. *Le Canada hier et aujourd'hui*. Toronto: Irwin, 1985.

Scott, Gail. "My Montréal: Notes of an Anglo-Québécois Writer." *Brick* 59 (Spring 1998): 4-9.

Scott, Marian. "Two Solitudes on Prevalence of French in Montreal: Poll." *Montreal Gazette* 22 June 2009.

Shirinian, Noémi. *La mosaïque comme métaphore de l'autre dans* Les Aurores montréales *de Monique Proulx*. M.A. thesis, Queen's University Kingston, 2001. 2 Sept. 2009 <http://www.collectionscanada.gc.ca/obj/s4/f2/dsk3/ftp04/MQ59402.pdf>.

Simon, Sherry. *Hybridité culturelle*. Montréal: L'île de la tortue, 1999.

-----. *Translating Montreal: Episodes in the Life of a Divided City*. Montreal: McGill-Queen's UP, 2006.

Sommer, Doris. Ed. *Bilingual Games: Some Literary Investigations*. NY: Palgrave Macmillan, 2003.

Spensley, Philip. "Franglo théâtre – esthétique et politique: Reaching Out to a Bilingual Audience, ou quoi ?" In *Cultural Identities in Canadian Literature*. Ed. Bénédicte Mauguière. NY: Lang, 1998. 163-72.

Statistics Canada. "2001 Census: Analysis Series – Profiles of Languages in Canada: English, French and Many Others." *Statcan.ca*. 2002. 19 Aug 2009 <http://www12.statcan.ca/english/census01/Products/Analytic/companion/lang/pdf/96F0030XIE2001005.pdf>.

Tabous sur l'histoire du Québec. Dir. Didier Deleskiewicz. La Sept/Arte, 2000.

Taylor, Charles. "Impediments to a Canadian Future." In *Reconciling the Solitudes: Essays on Canadian Federalism and Nationalism*. Ed. Guy Laforest. Montreal and Kingston: McGill-Queen's UP, 1993. 187-201.

Thacker, Robert. "Short Fiction." In *The Cambridge Companion to Canadian Literature*. Ed. Eva-Marie Kröller. Cambridge: Cambridge UP, 2004. 177-93.

"The Time of 'Two Solitudes' has passed: Jean." *CTV.ca*. 27 Sept. 2005. CTV globe media. 19 Aug. 2009 <http://www.ctv.ca/servlet/ArticleNews/story/CTVNews/20050927/governor_general_jean_050927/20050927?hub=TopStories>.

Tousignant, Pierre. "Constitutional Act, 1791." *The Canadian Encyclopedia*. 2009. Historica Foundation of Canada. 17 Aug. 2009 <http://www.thecanadianencyclopedia.com/index.cfm?PgNm=TCE&Params=A1ARTA0001872>.

Vaugeois, Denis. "Une langue sans statut." In *Le Français au Québec: 400 ans d'histoire et de vie*. Ed. Michel Plourde. Québec: Fides, 2003. 59-71.

Vigile. Bernard Frappier. 26 Oct. 2009 <http://www.vigile.net/>.

Vollmer, Helmut J. "Französisierung und Herkunftssprachen in Québec – Modelle und Perspektiven einer pluriethnischen Gesellschaft." *Grenzgänge* 3 (1995): 60-79.

Welsch, Wolfgang. "On the Acquisition and Possession of Commonalities." In *Transcultural English Studies: Theories, Fictions, Realities*. Eds. Frank Schulze-Engler and Sissy Helff. Amsterdam: Rodopi, 2009. 3-36.

-----. "Transkulturalität: Zur veränderten Verfassung heutiger Kulturen." In *Hybridkultur: Medien, Netze, Künste*. Eds. Irmela Schneider and Christian W. Thomsen. Köln: Wienand, 1997. 67-90.

Résumé

Une guerre particulière sévit dans la plus grande ville du Québec : on parle de « luttes linguistiques » à Montréal, où des Anglophones se regroupent dans la province par ailleurs majoritairement francophone. La dichotomie langagière se trouve au cœur de l'histoire culturelle de Montréal et elle reflète une relation pleine de tensions entre ce qu'on appelle les peuples fondateurs du Canada. Après la conquête, défaite et reconquête francophone, les deux communautés linguistiques ont enfin atteint un modus vivendi plus harmonieux au tournant du vingt-et-unième siècle.

Des écrivains se sont toujours engagés dans le débat et y ont apporté leur contribution. Mais comment la littérature contemporaine aborde-t-elle les relations anglaises-françaises des années après des événements cruciaux de l'histoire québécoise comme la Révolution tranquille, la crise d'Octobre, la mise en application de la Loi 101 et les deux référendums sur l'indépendance ? Neil Bissoondath et Monique Proulx, deux auteurs qui vivent et écrivent actuellement au Québec, ont examiné les interactions entre les Anglophones et les Francophones dans le Montréal d'aujourd'hui et ils ont fait passer de la mémoire culturelle dans leurs œuvres de fiction narrative. En lisant la littérature montréalaise comme une zone de contact, où le Moi rencontre l'Autre, nous verrons comment l'affrontement avec *the Other* modifie les deux partis impliqués, normalement pour le meilleur.

Dans le roman *Doing the Heart Good* de Bissoondath, le protagoniste et narrateur à la première personne Alistair Mackenzie fait défiler sa vie passée, pendant laquelle cet Anglophone monolingue ne pouvait fréquemment pas s'empêcher d'avoir affaire aux Francophones. Proulx met également ses personnages dans des situations dans lesquelles ils rencontrent de l'altérité et de l'aliénation dans son recueil de nouvelles *Les Aurores montréales*. Dans ses courts récits, outre l'Autre anglophone ou francophone, Proulx dépeint des migrants et leur participation à la dualité linguistique de Montréal. Bien que les deux textes ne soient pas ouvertement didactiques, Proulx et Bissoondath suggèrent tous les deux des moyens pour surmonter tous vestiges de l'antagonisme anglais-français historique et ils font la promotion d'une société québécoise effectivement multilingue et pluriethnique qui s'épanouit dans la différence.

Introduction

Les interactions entre Francophones et Anglophones au Québec apparaissent comme une relation de coopération et de confrontation. A la suite d'une double colonisation, d'abord française, puis britannique, les rapports entre les deux grands groupes linguistiques sont longtemps restés tendus dans la 'belle province.' Cependant dans la seconde moitié du vingtième siècle, la société québécoise s'est profondément transformée et nous pouvons parler d'un changement de paradigmes. Après une histoire relativement mouvementée on peut entrevoir un certain rapprochement entre les Franco- et les Anglo-Québécois au tournant du nouveau millénaire.

Cette étude vise à analyser le statu quo des relations entre Francophones et Anglophones comme elles se présentent dans la littérature montréalaise contemporaine. En examinant et comparant des œuvres choisies de fiction narrative écrites par Monique Proulx et Neil Bissoondath, deux auteurs qui vivent et écrivent actuellement au Québec, nous étudions la façon dont le sujet de la dichotomie anglais/français est traité en littérature. A cet égard il faut bien souligner que la littérature n'est pas un miroir de la réalité ; elle crée plutôt qu'elle ne représente. Après tout, le mot « fiction » dérive étymologiquement du latin *fingere* qui signifie « fabriquer », « façonner », « imaginer ». En outre, la littérature sélectionne, se focalise sur un aspect plutôt que sur un autre, parle de ceci mais se tait sur cela. Néanmoins elle peut servir de modèle pour mieux comprendre la réalité en décelant des structures de réalité.[386]

Dans le cadre de la présente étude nous mettons l'accent sur certains aspects culturels et sociolinguistiques qui apparaissent les plus pertinents pour la discussion de la dynamique francophone/anglophone au Québec. Cette analyse ne prétend cependant pas du tout être exhaustive, mais plutôt exemplaire et sélective. Comme le problème des « deux solitudes » se manifeste avant tout à Montréal, la ville la plus grande et la plus hétérogène du Québec où la majorité francophone est très fragile par rapport au reste du pays, la discussion se limitera aux textes qui se situent dans cette métropole québécoise. En nous basant sur des nouvelles extraites du recueil *Les aurores montréales* (1996) de Monique Proulx et sur le roman anglophone *Doing the Heart Good* (2002) de Neil Bissoondath, œuvres qui illustrent les interactions entre Francophones et Anglophones environ un demi-siècle après la Révolution tranquille au Québec, nous appréhendons la littérature montréalaise comme une zone de contact. De cette façon nous verrons comment l'affrontement entre le Moi et l'Autre affecte l'un et l'autre.

Contextualisation historique et socioculturelle

Tout d'abord, il faut replacer la discussion dans son contexte historique et socioculturel, car les problèmes d'aujourd'hui proviennent largement des inégalités d'hier. L'arrivée de Jacques Cartier en Gaspésie en 1534 marque le début de l'aventure coloniale française au Nouveau Monde. Quasiment pendant toute la domination fran-

---

[386] Cf. Thomas KLINKERT. *Einführung in die französische Literaturwissenschaft*. Berlin: Schmidt, 2004. 28-29.

çaise sur le territoire du Québec, celle-ci est contestée par les Anglais. Finalement, en 1759, les Français doivent se rendre après avoir été défaits par les troupes britanniques dans une bataille décisive sur les plaines d'Abraham.

Ainsi la majorité française est-elle transformée en peuple vaincu et il devient donc indispensable de trouver un mode de coexistence acceptable pour les deux communautés culturelles et linguistiques. Plusieurs lois sont votées pour régler les relations entre les rivaux historiques, comme par exemple l'Acte de Québec de 1774 qui, entre autres, reconnaît officiellement la langue française, réintègre l'usage du droit civil français et accorde aux Catholiques le droit de pratiquer leur religion. Néanmoins, ces mesures n'empêchent pas que les Canadiens français s'insurgent contre la domination anglaise, comme en 1837/38 dans la Rébellion des Patriotes au Bas-Canada. A la suite de cela, Lord Durham est nommé commissaire au Canada pour étudier la situation et dans son rapport de 1839 il parle de « deux nations en guerre au sein d'un même État », d'une lutte raciale et d'une haine mortelle divisant les habitants du Bas-Canada en deux groupes hostiles: Français et Anglais. Suite à ses recommandations principales, le Haut- et le Bas-Canada sont réunis pour former la Province du Canada-Uni. La population francophone se trouve ainsi dans une position minoritaire et, de plus, l'anglais est déclaré seule langue officielle, ce qui sera cependant révisé huit ans plus tard.

L'assimilation progressive des Canadiens français à la culture et à la langue anglaise ne s'effectue pas. Par contre, vu leur taux de natalité très élevé, les Francophones arrivent à contrebalancer la rapide augmentation de la population anglophone due à l'importante immigration en provenance de Grande-Bretagne ; ce phénomène est appelé « la revanche des berceaux ». L'état Canadien dans sa structure fédérale moderne est né en 1867 et à cette époque il est clair que la confédération signifie l'union des deux nations fondatrices du Canada, mais cette conception sera vivement controversée un siècle plus tard. Notamment dans les années 1980 et 1990, les débats constitutionnels semblent parvenir à leur paroxysme quand le statut de « société distincte » est explicitement dénié au Québec.

En ce qui concerne les relations entre Francophones et Anglophones au vingtième siècle, la Révolution tranquille des années 1960 et 1970 joue un rôle crucial. Les Francophones du Québec se soulèvent contre la domination anglaise afin de redevenir « maîtres chez eux », c'est-à-dire des citoyens égaux dans leur propre pays. En même temps qu'elle réussit à moderniser et restructurer la société québécoise et, de plus, à revaloriser la langue française, la majorité francophone du pays réévalue son rôle au sein de la province et du Canada. De surcroît, les Francophones de Québec ne se définissent plus comme « canadiens français » mais ils développent une identité et une conscience spécifiquement « québécoises ». Toutefois, aujourd'hui le terme « Québécois » ne désigne pas seulement les Francophones mais tous les habitants du Québec.

Quant à la langue, le Québec redevient une société effectivement francophone à partir des années 1970, surtout en vertu de la Loi 101 qui déclare le français seule langue officielle. Cet article de législation linguistique ne va naturellement pas sans déclencher beaucoup de tensions et de discussions, mais il aide à transformer le Québec en société d'accueil et à garantir la survivance de la langue française dans le contexte d'une majorité anglophone écrasante autant au Canada que sur le continent nord-américain en général.

Après les événements d'octobre 1970 et les deux référendums sur la souveraineté de 1980 et de 1995, les rapports parfois très difficiles entre le Québec et le Canada se sont de nouveau apaisés maintenant. D'ailleurs, les Anglo-Québécois se sont plus ou moins réconciliés avec la Loi 101 et ils ont également accepté, au moins la jeune génération, de ne plus être une minorité privilégiée. Cela ne veut pas dire qu'il n'y a plus de tensions entre les différentes communautés linguistiques. Cependant, ces tensions ont l'air de donner lieu à une immense fertilité créatrice au Québec, comme nous pouvons aisément nous en persuader en regardant l'extraordinaire originalité dont font preuve les écrivains québécois. Notre étude examine cette originalité dans des œuvres écrites environ vingt à trente ans après la promulgation de la fameuse Loi 101 et les deux référendums.

Deux perspectives littéraires

Des textes situés des deux côtés du clivage linguistique font l'objet de la présente investigation qui va permettre d'arriver à une analyse plus équilibrée de la dualité anglais/français. L'auteur francophone Monique Proulx et l'anglophone Neil Bissoondath – nés tous les deux dans les années 1950, l'une à Québec et l'autre à Trinidad – sont des représentants éminents de la scène culturelle et littéraire du Québec d'aujourd'hui. *Les Aurores montréales* de Proulx, paru en 1996, offre un microcosme littéraire et un portrait réaliste d'un Montréal multicolore couvrant approximativement la décade des années 1990. Comme les vingt-sept nouvelles du recueil se situent à Montréal, elles traitent naturellement aussi les interactions entre Francophones et Anglophones, notamment dans le récit éponyme « Les aurores montréales », dans « Oui or no » et dans la dernière nouvelle du livre « *Blanc* ». Dans *Doing the Heart Good*, un roman de Bissoondath publié en 2002, le protagoniste et narrateur à la première personne de soixante-quinze ans, Alistair Mackenzie, fait défiler sa vie passée après avoir perdu sa maison et toutes ses possessions à la suite d'un incendie. Ainsi cet Anglophone monolingue est-il contraint d'emménager chez sa fille, son gendre francophone bilingue et leur fils de six ans qui comprend l'anglais mais qui refuse de le parler. Au cours des épisodes du récit de Mackenzie, le lecteur fait la connaissance d'une véritable ménagerie de personnages divers, mais nous concentrons notre étude sur ses conflits avec son petit-fils François, son gendre Jacques et son voisin francophone Tremblay.

La voix francophone

Les courts récits des *Aurores montréales* ont en commun non seulement de se passer dans la ville de Montréal, mais aussi des ressemblances structurelles et stylistiques, et surtout l'ironie qui est apparemment le ton préféré de Proulx. En fait, l'humour caractérise la plupart de ses œuvres, même si Proulx aborde également des thèmes sombres comme la pauvreté, l'alcoolisme, le racisme, le déracinement et l'aliénation culturelle. En peignant la mosaïque de Montréal à la fin du vingtième siècle, le livre est peuplé de personnages très différents et autant de Francophones de souche que d'immigrés issus des quatre coins du monde.

C'est justement cette diversité qui déstabilise le protagoniste de la nouvelle « Les aurores montréales ». Laurel, un Francophone de souche de seize ans, s'impose la mission de maintenir un Montréal pur et francophone et il entretient une vision du multiculturalisme très étriquée, c'est-à-dire qu'il n'accepte le multiculturalisme que dans la mesure où celui-ci lui permet de profiter des épiceries et restaurants ethniques. Parcourant la ville pour amasser du matériel incriminant, Laurel s'applique à écrire un livre révélateur – « un vrai livre sur le vrai visage désolant du nouveau Montréal »,[387] annonce-t-il – qu'il va intituler *Les Aurores montréales*. La présence de son plus grand ennemi – l'anglais – est indéniable à Montréal et pour le moment Laurel doit se contenter d'écrire des phrases vengeresses dans son cahier rouge.

---

[387] PROULX, *AM*, 157.

L'altérité et l'étrangeté l'intimident fortement de sorte qu'il s'accroche à son cahier rouge, qui symbolise ses préjugés, pour se protéger contre tout ce qu'il ne comprend pas. Que Laurel apprécie si ardemment son héritage canadien français et qu'il dénigre tout ce qui est inconnu se laisse expliquer par le fait qu'il se trouve dans une crise identitaire. Manquant de repères, il se sent non seulement déconcerté mais réellement menacé par des signes d'appartenance, par exemple d'appartenance religieuse. Le tournant de la nouvelle est provoqué par l'affrontement ultime entre Laurel et son antagoniste, un adolescent d'origine grecque qui habite le même quartier et que Laurel appelle « Soufflaki » de manière condescendante. Alors que Laurel s'attend à une rencontre violente avec Soufflaki et sa « bande » qu'il n'a toujours considérés que comme ses ennemis, Soufflaki lui souhaite la bienvenue, car Laurel a récemment emménagé dans cette partie de la ville. Tout à coup Laurel se trouve dans la position de l'Autre, de l'envahisseur contre lequel il voulait défendre Montréal. En outre, Soufflaki le salue en français, ce qui montre que Laurel avait tort de croire que les immigrés constituent automatiquement un danger pour le Montréal francophone. A la fin, le protagoniste ne peut qu'admettre son ignorance, il jette donc son cahier rouge à la poubelle et décide de repartir à zéro. Nous pouvons donc parler de cette nouvelle comme d'un conte initiatique, car le récit retrace l'évolution et la maturation du jeune héros Laurel, qui est progressivement initié à la réalité de Montréal.

La nouvelle « Oui or no » a été décrite comme un « conte postmoderne sur le référendum de 1995 ».[388] Dans ce récit Proulx raconte l'histoire de la liaison entre la québécoise Éliane et l'anglophone Nick Rosenfeld de Toronto en établissant un parallèle entre leur relation amoureuse et les rapports entre le Québec et le Canada, qui ont été soumis à une épreuve particulière pendant l'époque du référendum sur l'indépendance québécoise de 1995. Même si Éliane et Nick Rosenfeld vivent des moments extraordinairement passionnés malgré la barrière linguistique et la communication très limitée qui l'accompagne, leur relation semble vouée à l'échec dès le début. Premièrement, ils se trouvent dans une situation plutôt inégale, car ils ne se parlent que dans la langue de Nick Rosenfeld ; par ailleurs, il n'y a pas beaucoup d'échange verbal puisqu'ils ne se comprennent pas vraiment. Ensuite, en partageant la couche de Nick Rosenfeld Éliane trompe son partenaire Philippe qu'elle appelle aussi affectueusement Filippo. Celui-ci est un partisan ardent de la cause souverainiste du Québec et quand Éliane commence à tout traduire mentalement dans la

---

[388] FISHER, 313.

langue de Nick Rosenfeld afin de mieux le comprendre, elle ressent beaucoup plus qu'elle trahit Filippo qu'avec seulement son amant de Toronto. Et puis, Éliane se rend compte peu à peu qu'elle n'est rien de spécial dans la vie de Nick Rosenfeld, ce qui est comparable au rôle du Québec au Canada, puisqu'il n'est qu'une province parmi neuf autres. A la fin, après le résultat du référendum décevant pour Filippo, Éliane et la majorité des Franco-Québécois, Nick Rosenfeld renoue le contact avec Éliane et lui téléphone pour s'excuser. Etant donné que « Oui or no » compare métaphoriquement la liaison d'Éliane avec la relation entre le Québec et le Canada, le fait que Nick Rosenfeld demande pardon à Éliane peut être interprété à plusieurs niveaux. D'un côté, ses excuses se rapportent à la déception amoureuse d'Éliane, mais de l'autre, nous pouvons les voir comme un geste conciliant du Canada pour montrer qu'il reconnaît la déception idéologique du Québec même s'il ne la comprend pas tout à fait. Cette reconnaissance est cruciale si nous considérons que le dynamisme séparatiste était pratiquement motivé au premier chef par un manque de reconnaissance. Cette nouvelle illustre donc les relations ambiguës entre les Francophones du Québec et les Canadiens anglophones d'autres provinces autour des événements du référendum où le « non » l'a remporté de justesse contre le « oui » des souverainistes.

Si « Oui or no » traite les rapports entre le Québec et le Canada, la dernière nouvelle des *Aurores montréales*, « *Blanc* », traite les interactions entre les Francophones et les Anglophones à l'intérieur du Québec. « *Blanc* » est le dernier récit d'une série de six nouvelles contenant des couleurs dans leurs titres (les autres s'appellent « *Gris et blanc* », « *Jaune et blanc* », « *Rose et blanc* », « *Noir et blanc* », « *Rouge et blanc* »). Ces nouvelles se distinguent d'abord typographiquement des autres contes, car elles sont écrites en italiques, ensuite la narration est à la première personne, souvent sous forme d'une lettre. D'ailleurs, trois de ces récits sont dédiés aux auteurs néo-québécois – à savoir à Ying Chen (« *Jaune et blanc* »), à Marco Micone (« *Rose et blanc* ») et à Dany Laferrière (« *Noir et blanc* ») – et ils foisonnent de références intertextuelles. A travers ces six nouvelles, Proulx fait le point sur la diversité et l'hybridité urbaine de Montréal ; dans les cinq premières, elle met en scène des immigrés apportant leurs couleurs individuelles à Montréal et elle montre comment ces « autres solitudes » participent à la pluralité langagière de la ville. Par contre, la nouvelle « *Blanc* » dépeint la relation entre une Francophone et un Anglophone, les représentants des fameuses « deux solitudes » de Montréal. Le titre de ce récit ne contient pas d'autre couleur parce que « *Blanc* » renonce finalement aux catégorisations comme « anglophone » ou « montréalais » et que Montréal, comme la couleur blanche qui est à la fois l'absence et la présence de toutes les couleurs du spectre, absorbe et mélange une grande variété de gens et d'ethnicités pour devenir « un espace vierge »[389] où le Moi et l'Autre se rejoignent et fusionnent. « *Blanc* » raconte l'histoire d'une jeune femme francophone qui retourne à Montréal après avoir quitté la ville après l'échec du référendum de 1995. La nouvelle décrit l'évolution de la femme qui se trouve au début profondément désorientée dans la métropole à son retour, mais qui se réconcilie avec elle-même et avec sa vie à Montréal au cours de sa relation avec l'anglophone Mister Murphy. Celui-ci est sur le point de mourir et la protagoniste qui s'est engagée dans un programme bénévole de soins palliatifs se porte volontaire pour accompagner cet homme inconnu pendant les derniers moments de sa vie. Aussitôt que les deux personnages principaux de ce récit entrent en contact, ils cessent d'être des étrangers l'un pour l'autre. De plus, ils découvrent que les choses qui les divisent, qui opposent des groupes comme les Franco- et les Anglo-Montréalais, sont insignifiantes en comparaison avec leurs points communs et qu'il peut être très libérateur de rencontrer l'Autre sans préjugés, c'est-à-dire impartialement et sans vouloir l'étiqueter comme ceci ou cela. L'idée de la page blanche est surtout développée à la fin, quand la protagoniste se sent comme une *tabula rasa* prête à réécrire son histoire, et elle implique qu'il faut aussi ouvrir une nouvelle page pour écrire une nouvelle histoire des relations entre Francophones et Anglophones à Montréal. Bref, nous pouvons constater que « *Blanc* » est un récit de formation de la protagoniste aussi bien que de la ville de Montréal de la période post-référendaire.

La voix anglophone

Doing the Heart Good de Bissoondath est également une sorte de roman d'apprentissage. Vers la fin de sa vie, Alistair Mackenzie décide de rédiger ses mémoires pour éviter de sombrer dans l'oubli. Par ce processus au cours duquel il passe en revue son existence, cet homme sûr de ses opinions et de ses attitudes acquiert finalement un savoir qui lui a été dénié tout au long de sa vie. De plus, il écrit ce récit autobiographique dans le but de le léguer à son petit-fils pour que celui-ci comprenne mieux ses origines familiales. C'est en outre une façon de créer un lien durable avec son petit-fils François en dépit de leur différence langagière. Le grand-père de soixante-quinze et le petit-fils de six ans sont tous les deux très opiniâtres ; l'un fait

---

[389] PROULX, *AM*, 239.

semblant de ne pas comprendre le français et refuse de le parler alors que l'autre comprend l'anglais mais préfère ne jamais le parler. Pourtant, cela n'empêche pas le narrateur à la fin du roman d'envisager un avenir commun pour lui et son petit-fils.

L'obstination n'est qu'un des traits distinctifs d'Alistair Mackenzie. En général, ce professeur retraité se caractérise par son égocentrisme – ceci est particulièrement évident dans le fait qu'il considère toujours son avis comme le meilleur –, son aversion pour les changements et sa conception du monde relativement rigide. C'est seulement en prenant du recul pour raconter sa vie que le protagoniste réussit à se comprendre finalement mieux lui-même ainsi que les gens qui ont influencé sa vie. Mais Mackenzie ne cherche certainement pas de bon gré à obtenir toutes ces révélations qu'il vit vers la fin de sa vie et à réviser ses opinions ; il est effectivement forcé à trouver son bonheur. Par exemple, il s'oppose avec véhémence à emménager chez sa fille et ce n'est qu'après que sa maison est détruite qu'il y consent. Faisant partie d'un foyer biculturel, Mackenzie ne peut ainsi pas éviter d'interagir avec son gendre Jacques dont il anglicise le nom : « Jack ». D'abord, ces deux personnages illustrent les malentendus qui existent entre leurs groupes culturels respectifs et leurs visions divergentes de l'histoire. Peu à peu Mackenzie se rend compte de son ignorance, de sa « myopie » culturelle et de l'importance de la langue pour chaque individu. En effet, il commence à comprendre la ferveur pour leur langue des Francophones de Montréal et leurs soucis en ce qui concerne la survivance du français. A la fin, le narrateur fait même l'effort de prononcer le nom de son gendre correctement.

Tout au long de sa vie, Mackenzie résiste à de tels changements et il préfère s'immerger dans le passé, c'est-à-dire dans les souvenirs d'une existence cloisonnée ou bien à l'abri du monde réel et exempte de tout conflit. Au cours du récit, mémoire individuelle et collective sont fréquemment juxtaposées bien que la narration s'intéresse avant tout aux expériences personnelles du protagoniste. Celui-ci, né en 1920, a vécu presque tous les événements principaux dans le Québec du vingtième siècle à propos de la dichotomie francophone/anglophone, notamment la transformation de la société québécoise lors de la Révolution tranquille et l'émancipation subséquente des Québécois francophones. Néanmoins, Mackenzie se sent supérieur par rapport aux Francophones en vertu de l'hégémonie anglophone historique au Québec et il ignore simplement tous ces changements qui pourraient remettre en question sa version imaginée des relations de pouvoir à Montréal. A ce sujet nous devons considérer que le narrateur vit toute sa vie à Montréal sans jamais parler ou vouloir apprendre la langue de la majorité. C'est un des paradoxes de l'espace urbain qu'on puisse partager le même territoire géopolitique sans parler la langue de l'autre, puisque la proximité n'entraîne pas nécessairement l'intimité ou l'interaction. Cependant, Mackenzie ne peut éviter d'interagir avec son voisin francophone Tremblay qui habite la même maison. Les deux hommes antithétiques représentent de façon évidente les communautés culturelles et linguistiques auxquelles ils appartiennent. Donc, leurs querelles sont emblématiques de la division anglais/français. Il faut toutefois ajouter que leur relation n'est tendue que du côté de Mackenzie, car Tremblay est un voisin affable et complaisant. Le narrateur méprise tout le temps Tremblay et le traite comme une intrusion intempestive dans sa vie. Seulement à la fin il devient clair que leurs disputes ne sont que superficielles et qu'il s'agit là plutôt d'un jeu. En fait, Mackenzie s'amuse de son rôle qui lui permet de s'indigner sans cesse contre Tremblay auquel il assigne le rôle de son antagoniste francophone. A travers un événement franchement symbolique – un incendie causé par des jeunes anglophones qui mettent le feu au fleur-de-lis de Tremblay le vingt-quatre juin, la fête nationale du Québec – Bissoondath provoque le rapprochement ultime entre ces deux personnages. Dans leur conversation à la fin du roman indiquant une amitié éventuelle, Mackenzie et Tremblay se mettent d'accord sur une nouvelle manière de se parler et sur l'oubli de leur ancien antagonisme.

Alistair Mackenzie a toujours essayé d'éviter la communication interculturelle et interlinguistique, mais en ratant cette tentative il réussit finalement à se réconcilier avec son environnement. A peu près de la même façon que les personnages des nouvelles de Proulx, le protagoniste et narrateur du roman de Bissoondath atteint une connaissance plus profonde de la vie et aussi de la réalité pluraliste de Montréal grâce à ses expériences avec l'Autre. Rappelons à cet égard les mots de Julia Kristeva : « A partir de l'autre, je me réconcilie avec ma propre altérité-étrangeté ».[390] Cette valorisation de l'altérité qui est suggérée dans *Doing the Heart Good* aussi bien que dans *Les Aurores montréales* révèle effectivement certains des changements positifs survenus à Montréal dans les années post-référendaires.

Conclusion

Bien sûr, les deux solitudes ne sont pas (encore) métamorphosées en deux sollicitudes, mais il y a plusieurs indices qui dénotent une évolution favorable dans l'état

---

[390] KRISTEVA, 269.

des relations entre Francophones et Anglophones à Montréal à l'aube du nouveau millénaire. Aujourd'hui, les Québécois francophones ont plus d'assurance qu'avant les années 1990 et il y a de plus en plus d'échange et d'interaction entre les Anglophones et les Francophones. Les exemples de littérature montréalaise contemporaine, que ce soit en français ou en anglais, que nous venons d'étudier reflètent ces tendances. Nous avons analysé comment les textes s'approprient la mémoire collective, comment ils traduisent la pluralité de Montréal et provoquent des affrontements entre personnages de différentes communautés ethniques et linguistiques qui aboutissent finalement à un rapprochement réel de ces groupes. De cette façon nous avons pu nous faire une idée de la situation culturelle et sociolinguistique du Montréal contemporain. En résumé, nous pouvons donner raison à Sherry Simon quand elle parle d'un nouveau Montréal[391] depuis les années post-référendaires – un Montréal aux relations sociales beaucoup plus détendues qui est habité par des Anglo- et Franco-Montréalais, des individus souvent bilingues ou même trilingues qui se réjouissent de la diversité de la métropole.

---

[391] Cf. SIMON (2006), 8, 10.

ibidem-Verlag

Melchiorstr. 15

D-70439 Stuttgart

info@ibidem-verlag.de

www.ibidem-verlag.de
www.ibidem.eu
www.edition-noema.de
www.autorenbetreuung.de